Essays in Real Estate Research
Band 10

Edited by
N. B. Rottke, Eschborn, Germany
J. Mutl, Wiesbaden, Germany

Die Reihe „Essays in Real Estate Research", herausgegeben von Professor Dr. Nico B. Rottke FRICS und Professor Jan Mutl, Ph.D. umfasst aktuelle Forschungsarbeiten der Promovenden der Lehrstühle und Professuren des Real Estate Management Institutes der EBS Business School. Forschungs- und Lehrschwerpunkte des Institutes bilden die interdisziplinären Aspekte der Immobilientransaktion sowie die nachhaltige Wertschöpfungskette im Immobilienlebenszyklus. Die Kapitalmärkte werden als essenzieller Bestandteil der Entwicklung der Immobilienmärkte aufgefasst.

Die in der Regel empirischen Studien betrachten transaktions- und kapitalmarktnahe Themenbereiche aus dem Blickwinkel der institutionellen Immobiliengewerbe- und -wohnungswirtschaft, wie bspw. Finanzierung, Kapitalmarktstruktur, Investition, Risikomanagement, Bewertung, Ökonomie oder Portfoliomanagement, aber auch angewandte Themen wie Corporate Real Estate Management, Projektentwicklung oder Unternehmensführung. Die ersten 11 Bände der Reihe erschienen bis 2014 auch im Immobilien Manager Verlag, Köln.

The series "Essays in Real Estate Research", published by Professor Dr. Nico B. Rottke FRICS and Professor Jan Mutl, Ph.D., includes current research work of doctoral students at the chairs and professorships of the Real Estate Management Institute of EBS Business School. The research and teaching focus of the Institute constitutes the interdisciplinary aspects of real estate transactions as well as the sustainable value creation chain within the real estate life cycle. The capital markets are regarded as essential components of the development of the real estate markets.

The mostly empirical studies consider transactional as well as capital market topics from the point of view of the institutional commercial and residential real estate industry, such as finance, capital market structure, investment, risk management, valuation, economics or portfolio management, but also applied topics such as corporate real estate management, real estate development, or leadership issues in the property industry. The first 11 volumes of the series appeared up until 2014 in Immobilien Manager Publishing, Cologne, as well.

Edited by
Nico B. Rottke
Ernst & Young Real Estate GmbH
Eschborn, Germany

Jan Mutl
Real Estate Management Institute
EBS Business School
Wiesbaden, Germany

Nicolai C. Striewe

Corporate Governance of Real Estate Investment Trusts

With a Preface of the Editors by
Prof. Dr. Nico B. Rottke and Prof. Dr. Matthias Thomas

Springer Gabler

Dr. Nicolai C. Striewe
EBS Business School
Wiesbaden, Germany

Unchanged Reprint 2016

Up to 2014 the title was published in Immobilien Manager Verlag, Cologne, in the series „Schriftenreihe zur immobilienwirtschaftlichen Forschung“.

Essays in Real Estate Research
ISBN 978-3-658-11618-7 ISBN 978-3-658-11619-4 (eBook)
DOI 10.1007/978-3-658-11619-4

Library of Congress Control Number: 2015955834

Springer Gabler
Previously published by Immobilien Manager Verlag, Cologne, 2013

Printed on acid-free paper

Springer Gabler is a brand of Springer Fachmedien Wiesbaden
Springer Fachmedien Wiesbaden is part of Springer Science+Business Media
(www.springer.com)

Preface of the Editors

The dissertation of Dr. Nicolai Striewe covers three issues related to the governance of real estate investment trusts (REITs). Each of these issues is dealt with in a separate essay. The essays are empirical in nature and draw on U.S. data. However, the conclusions are relevant not only for the governance of U.S. REITs but for REITs in general, given that REITs in other countries are closely modeled after those in the U.S. Focusing his research on the U.S. is, therefore, a sensible strategy for Dr. Striewe because there is a lot to learn from the American experience, in terms of both positive and negative aspects of REIT governance. Choosing to base the analysis on U.S. data makes all the more sense given that the U.S. REIT market is so far the only well developed REIT market in the world and the only one that has reliable data over many years.

From a policy perspective, the work of Dr. Striewe is highly relevant given the problems of governance we have seen in the wake of the mortgage crisis and, later, the financial and economic crisis. The issue of how to contain or rein in CEOs and other corporate officers for the longer benefit of investors and other stakeholders of public companies is of very significant importance. Arguably, the recent economic crisis is intimately tied to the breakdown of effective corporate governance structures. Yet change has been slow to emerge, if at all. Providing aspiring MBAs with a course in ethics or in social responsibility is unlikely to resolve the issue of governance. What is needed are effective mechanisms to contain CEOs and their fellow managers. In his dissertation Dr. Striewe is looking at two such mechanisms in the context of REITS: external versus internal management and institutional ownership.

The few studies that cover these topics have potentially serious methodological shortcomings or rely on data that make causal analysis difficult if not impossible. The three essays contained in Dr. Striewe's dissertation advance the literature in both respects. The data are richer, in that panel data are used, and more thoroughly motivated than in the previous work. Hence, they hold the promise for more representative results. The three essays also stand out relative to the published research in that fixed-effects panel data estimators are used. In contrast to the common cross-sectional approach, the results of the papers are more reliable because they can be more easily interpreted as causal and independent of unobserved confounding factors.

The first two chapters provide a very readable overview of the dissertation and the topic of corporate governance, as it related to economic theory on the one hand and the institutional environment of REITs on the other.

The first essay, which makes up chapter 3 of the dissertation, was published in the Journal of Real Estate Research. This journal is one of the top three academic journals in the world devoted to research in the field of real estate.

The paper looks into the external advisor structure of REITs and its impact on the capital structure of REITs. For the early REIT era, when REITs received little attention or scrutiny from stock market participants, previous research associated externally advised REITs with an excessive leverage, which translates into a higher bankruptcy risk. Dr. Striewe does a good job explaining the rational for the high leverage values; in particular how they may follow from the compensation structure of externally advised REITs. In the new REIT era, which is typically thought to have begun around the middle of the 1990s, REITs have moved from being an exotic corporate structure on the sidelines of the stock market to becoming main stream. The question that appears to have not been asked is whether externally advised REITs continue to behave the way they did in the early REIT era, that is, excessively driving up their leverage ratios.

The study makes use of time fixed-effects to account for macroeconomic changes and other effects that are common to all REITs. In addition, fixed-effects are utilized for the different property types that REITs specialize in.

The main result of the paper is opposite to the conventional wisdom, which still relies on studies and results focused on the early REIT era. In particular, the study finds that externally advised REITs choose a lower leverage compared to their internally advised counterparts. This conclusion is fully consistent with the fact that externally advised REITs bear higher costs of debt. It suggests that there is no agency conflict any more for externally advised REITs along the lines suggested in the literature for the early REIT era.

The second essay, chapter 4, was published in the Journal of Real Estate Portfolio Management, another highly ranked real estate research journal. The essay analyses the impact that institutional investors have had on the performance on REITs. Institutional investors tend to be more informed about the companies they invest in than individual investors. They also tend to have significantly more influence on corporate policy. Both facts can make institutional investors into a useful countervailing power relative to corporate managers who are overly interested in serving their own interests.

Similar to the first paper, the study makes use of a panel data set for U.S. REITs. Firm fixed-effects are employed to account for unobserved heterogeneity. The focus is on measuring the impact of both the level and the change in institutional ownership on market performance, as measured by Tobin's Q, and on accounting performance, as measured by returns on assets. One of the key innovations over the existing literature is the focus on the interactions between the change in institutional ownership and several measures of corporate governance. This appears to be a sensible step forward in the research effort to pin down the performance impact of more institutional monitoring and control.

Particularly noteworthy in the paper is the careful discussion of the estimation results in section 4.4. Numerous robustness checks are presented and alternative explanations of the results are evaluated in a way that lets the reader come away with the impression that the analysis has been conducted in a very thoughtful way.

The third paper, which is single-authored, is an outgrowth of the second paper. If institutional investors can improve the bottom line of REITs, then it may be in the interest of REITs to attract them. Dr. Striewe asks two important practical questions in this context. First, what role do macroeconomic conditions play for institutional investors when they consider investing in REITs? Second, what types of REIT characteristics are favored by institutional investors? An answer to these questions is of immediate policy relevance for REITs.

Although a number of studies have tried to isolate the driving forces behind the interest of institutional investors in REITs, they suffer from two important problems. First and foremost, they rely on cross-sectional data, which makes it difficult to identify causal effects. Second, macroeconomic factors are not explicitly considered. This is one reason why existing studies are troubled by mixed results, in particular, period-specific factors, that is, the macroeconomic environment, play a significant role.

Of particular note in the paper is its careful attention to detail in the construction of the panel data set. This is very evident, for example, in the way the Livingstone Survey data are incorporated and in how the microeconomic variables are defined. As in papers one and two, excellent use is made of the fixed-effects estimator to check that the chosen macroeconomic factors truly capture the data generating process of institutional ownership of REITs. In terms of methodology, the variance decomposition presented in Table 18 is helpful in sorting out the relative importance of the driving forces behind institutional investment.

We consider all three essays to be excellent studies relative to the published empirical research on governance issues, be they focused on REITs or corporations in general. The essays are well motivated, very timely and of immediate policy relevance. They are based on very detailed data work, display excellent methodological choices, and are very well researched in terms of the existing academic literature. The doctoral thesis more than fulfills the requirements and reflects the state-of-the-art of empirical research on REIT governance issues. It deservedly received a summa cum laude evaluation in March 2012.

Wiesbaden, July 30, 2013

Prof. Dr. Nico B. Rottke FRICS CRE

Executive Vice-President, EBS Universität für Wirtschaft und Recht

Head of Institute, Real Estate Management Institute, EBS Business School

Aareal Endowed Chair of Real Estate Investment & Finance

&

Prof. Dr. Matthias Thomas MRICS

Endowed Chair of Real Estate Management, EBS Business School

Preface of the Author

This dissertation was motivated by the events surrounding the recent global financial crisis that started in 2008 following the subprime mortgage crisis. The financial crisis led to massive government intervention to rescue the economy and compensate for excessive risk-taking by managers.

Why did many executives engage in risky strategies from a behavioral point of view? The reason is that many managers tended to maximize their own benefit rather than shareholder value. This was made possible by the fact that both parties tend to have different incentives.

Incentive structures have changed a great deal in recent decades due to market deregulation and financial innovation. This change, in part, created distorted incentives, which in turn provoked opportunistic managerial behavior. One of the key changes relates to compensation: it has become increasingly performance-linked. The focus has shifted to short-term success at the expense of sustainable performance. Empirical examples of the results are corporate scandals, deceptive accounting and fraudulent managerial actions. And yet, even in the face of failure, CEOs have received golden parachutes and generous bonus payments. Therefore public attention is now focused on the compensation levels of top executives - and this scrutiny appears to be at an all-time high. It is apparent to us that corporate governance has failed in this context.

Corporate governance finds its most cited definition in the article "A Survey of

Corporate Governance" by Shleifer and Vishny, which appeared in the Journal of Finance in 1997. Since that article appeared, the topic has expanded greatly and become truly interdisciplinary. Researchers not only from the fields of economics and finance but also from the disciplines of law, management, and accounting now cover the topic. Corporate governance appeared as a keyword in more than a thousand SSRN abstracts in 2011.

Research on corporate governance builds on one major theory: the principle-agent theory. This theory substantiates the need for corporate governance. It describes how managers may consume perks, make selfish risk choices and focus on short-term profits at the expense of long-term gains. Such agency costs can materialize from the conflicts of interests between the principal, namely the shareholder, and the agent, namely the manager.

Hence, my dissertation is about a problem that we all know. But the solution is not clear at all. What is certain is that corporate governance mechanisms are an important piece of the puzzle.

I have always been interested in questions about why people behave as they do, be it in business, in politics or in private life. Rather than viewing an enterprise as a sum of its assets, I prefer to focus on the people within the firm. The reason is that the behavior of firms is a function of the decision-making of individuals who follow their individual incentives. Firms are only maximizing shareholder wealth if the utility functions of the people within the firm are consistent with the shareholder's wealth maximization objective. The separation of ownership and control in most firms induces agency issues, which stem from conflicts of interest and incentive problems. Resulting opportunistic behavior can become so serious that it adversely impacts corporate performance.

This dissertation brings forward new evidence on the impact of conflicts of interests in the real estate market and focuses on an important, but less visible corporate governance mechanism, namely institutional monitoring. Institutional monitoring moderates the actions of managers and encourages value-maximizing decisions for the benefit of the shareholder. Institutional investors utilize a wide set of instruments to monitor managerial actions, including direct influence through personal correspondence with the management, leading proxy fights to achieve larger goals or threatening to vote with their feet if they feel dissatisfied with the management.

Corporate governance is essential to all parts of the economy. But why is it so important for the real estate market, in particular the market for REITs? The REIT exhibits characteristics that can become problematic with respect to corporate governance. Here are a few: First, only a few REITs are assessed by rating agencies and covered by analysts. This cancels out two important monitoring institutions. Second, the function of the market for corporate control is weak for REITs, because ownership restrictions in the REIT market act as a take-over defense. Third, leverage policies of REITs in the US are not legally capped at a set threshold level. This leaves the REIT manager with considerable freedom.

The effective study of principal-agent conflicts and institutional monitoring requires a mature REIT market to draw general conclusions that apply for REIT markets all over the world. Only the US market provides an unmatched data quality with a long time series and a large cross-section for REITs. It is the largest and most efficient securitized real estate market worldwide. This is crucial for applying robust panel data models to obtain reliable causal inferences. The National Association of Real Estate Investment Trusts estimates that the Equity REIT market represents about $ 544 billion of the North American commercial property market (about $ 7 trillion) as of 2012. REITs are liquid and investors have no minimum investment requirement. The REIT structure benefits from special tax considerations and is legally required to pay out income. These characteristics make the REIT an ideal subject for a corporate governance study.

The paper of chapter three, "Corporate Governance and the Leverage of REITs: The Impact of the Advisor Structure" was published in the Journal of Real Estate Research, Vol. 35, No. 1, 2013. Earlier versions of the paper were presented at the 16th conference of the European Real Estate Society (ERES) in Stockholm, Sweden, in 2009 and at the 26th conference of the American Real Estate Society (ARES) in Naples, Florida, USA, in 2010. A later version of the paper in chapter four was published under the title "The Impact of Institutional Ownership on REIT Performance" in the Journal of Real Estate Portfolio Management, Vol. 19, No. 1, 2013. The paper of chapter five, "What Drives Institutions to Invest in REITs?", was presented at the 28th conference of the ARES in St. Petersburg, Florida, USA. I am grateful for the helpful comments I received from the conference participants and the journals' reviewers.

In the following I would like to express thanks to important contributors. Sincere thanks to my academic supervisors Professor Dr. Nico B. Rottke FRICS CRE from EBS University, Wiesbaden, and Professor Dr. Joachim Zietz from Middle Tennessee State University, USA, for their unwavering support. They continuously provided me with valuable advice and motivating guidance throughout my entire doctoral studies. Special thanks to my academic advisors Professor Randy I. Anderson PhD CRE from the University of Central Florida, USA, and Professor John L. Glascock PhD FRICS from the University of Connecticut, USA, for their helpful comments and insights on my research. Many thanks to my colleagues at the Real Estate Management Institute of the European Business School (EBS) University, who made the time during my doctoral studies a memorable and enriching experience, academically as well as personally. I greatly appreciate being part of the broad support network of EBS University.

My greatest gratitude is reserved for my parents: for believing in me and providing me the freedom and unconditional support to choose my direction in life and pursue my academic preferences, which culminated in my doctoral studies at EBS University.

Wiesbaden, July 30, 2013

Nicolai C. Striewe

Table of Contents

List of Figures

List of Tables

List of Abbreviations

AMEX	American Stock Exchange
CAPM	Capital Asset Pricing Model
CEO	Chief Executive Officer
CFO	Chief Financial Officer
CPI	Consumer Price Index
CRSP	Center for Research in Security Prices
GDP	Gross Domestic Product
IO	Institutional Ownership
IPO	Initial Public Offering
IRS	Internal Revenue Service
NYSE	New York Stock Exchange
OLS	Ordinary Least Squares
R&D	Research and Development
REIT	Real Estate Investment Trust
REOC	Real Estate Operating Company
ROA	Return on Assets
SD	Standard Deviation
SEC	Securities Exchange Commission
SIC	Security Identification Code
SOX	Sarbanes-Oxley Act
TIPS	Treasury Inflation-Protected Securities

1 Introduction

1.1 Motivation and Problem Definition

While corporate governance has received extensive coverage in the finance literature, associated research on real estate investment trusts (REITs) still lacks studies on principal-agent conflicts (agency conflicts) and corporate governance mechanisms. This thesis analyzes potential opportunistic behavior of REIT managers and provides empirical evidence on the effectiveness of institutional monitoring as a corporate governance mechanism. It also suggests ways to promote sustainable management by means of institutional participation. The results of the study provide valuable insights to enhance corporate governance, transparency and efficiency in the REIT market. They encourage (a) academics to include a behavioral component into studies of the REIT market, (b) REIT managers to incorporate effective monitoring and control mechanisms, (c) investors to become more aware of agency conflicts in REITs and (d) policy makers to facilitate a legal framework conducive to a sustainable REIT market.

To achieve these objectives, this thesis studies corporate governance issues of REITs from a number of different perspectives. The research gaps and our motivation to fill these gaps are explained in the following pages and are divided into three elements. These are later treated as separate research papers.

In step one, we identify where agency conflicts and associated underperformance were apparent in the past: in the capital structure of externally advised REITs. We take a look at how misaligned compensation schemes could induce managers to choose leverage opportunistically twenty years ago. Of current interest is the development of agency issues over time; in particular, whether the REIT market has managed to resolve previous agency conflicts through a more refined corporate governance structure. Our empirical findings could help investors regain confidence in externally advised REITs, which forfeited credibility in the past. The study's implications intend to give academics, REIT managers, investors and policy makers feedback on how well the REIT market has adopted key features of corporate governance.

In a second step, after having analyzed an agency conflict that is unique to the REIT market, we look at a general mechanism to alleviate agency conflicts: institutional monitoring. We analyze to what extent institutional investors can contribute towards establishing corporate governance principles in the REIT sector. Although the theoretical role of institutions for REITs is clear in the literature, it is not verified empirically whether the positive performance impact of institutional engagement is related to corporate governance. Empirical support for such inference could (1) give academics an explanation for puzzling abnormal returns when ownership changes, (2) motivate REIT managers to engage in relationships with institutions, (3) encourage institutional investors to engage in monitoring and corporate control activities and (4) provide policy makers with an incentive to foster institutional participation with the aim to alleviate agency conflicts and promote corporate governance.

In a third step, we develop a guide for REIT managers to attract institutional investors with the aim of fostering corporate governance and to better understand the investment considerations of institutional investors in the REIT market. The limited research on the motivations of institutional investors focuses narrowly on firm size and liquidity. However, the reasons that drive institutions to invest in REITs are likely more complicated and include macroeconomic factors as well as REIT characteristics. Better knowledge of what motivates institutional investors can familiarize REIT managers with institutional expectations and enable them to adjust their business decisions accordingly.

Based on these research gaps we have prepared three individual research papers that address the tripodal focus of the thesis. The papers contribute to the existing body of the academic literature on corporate governance, a topic that has received considerable interest from industry and academia. How the papers are structured and what methodology we use to address the research problems is briefly outlined in the following section.

1.2 Outline of Dissertation

The remainder of the dissertation comprises a theoretical background and review of the literature on corporate governance and REITs, three research papers that cover corporate governance in real estate investment trusts and a conclusion. The following explains how the thesis is structured.

Chapter two covers the theoretical background and reviews the literature on corporate governance and REITs. First, the chapter introduces corporate governance and the associated agency theory in a general finance context. Second, the relevance of the topics is highlighted against the background of the historical development of financial markets with special reference to recent market distortions. We then discuss corporate governance in the REIT context; in particular, the special features of REITs and how they add to the identification strategies implemented by the three papers.

Paper one (chapter three) addresses the agency problems involved in externally advised REITs and relates them to opportunistic capital structure choices. It provides new insight on the impact of the advisor structure on leverage for the new REIT era (since 1993), that is, for the period following the conversion of the majority of externally advised REITs to internally advised REITs.[1] Our study uses data on 265 US REITs from 1994 to 2010 to test whether the charges brought upon externally advised REITs regarding agency issues and associated underperformance during the old REIT era (1981-1992) still exist today in the new REIT era. The potential for opportunistic behavior arose from misaligned compensation schemes.

The paper starts out with an introduction that motivates the research problem by highlighting the peculiarities and special incentive structures of REIT advisor types. Next, we provide a theoretical background of the relevant theories of capital structure as they relate to corporate governance and associated empirical findings. The dataset is described before the identification strategy is discussed. The next section presents the empirical findings and their interpretation. The conclusion summarizes the major findings and explains their economic relevance.

---

[1] The majority of the conversions took place in the years following the Tax Reform Act of 1986, which allowed REITs to operate and self-manage properties.

Paper two (chapter four) analyzes whether institutional investors can influence agency conflicts in securitized real estate via monitoring and shareholder activism. The paper examines the performance impact of institutional investment that is related to corporate governance. The study employs panel data of 250 firms for the period 1998Q1 to 2010Q4. The identification strategy makes use of Fama MacBeth regressions to measure the performance impact of the level and change in institutional ownership and their interactions with proxies of corporate governance. The models take factors for market, size, book-to-market and momentum effects into account as suggested by Fama and French (1992) and Carhart (1997).

This paper first presents the questions that motivate the study and how they contribute to the literature. Next, the literature and its associated findings, which shape the theoretical background for this chapter, are reviewed. This is followed by a description of the dataset and the empirical methodology. The estimation results are presented next. Sensitivity analyses test for robustness of the model results and consider alternative interpretations. The chapter concludes with a summary of the study's most important results.

Paper three (chapter five) addresses an issue that follows from paper two: the macroeconomic and microeconomic factors that motivate institutional investors to invest in REITs. In particular, we ask two questions: "Under what macroeconomic circumstances do institutions choose REITs?" and "Do changes in REIT characteristics drive institutional investment and disinvestment over time?" To answer these two questions we use quarterly panel data of 136 US REITs for the period 2000 to 2010. The identification strategy applies the firm fixed-effects estimator and variance decompositions. Knowing the preferences of institutional investors is instrumental to successfully operate REITs and to improve corporate governance by institutional monitoring of the management. REITs could tailor operating and financial characteristics to a particular institutional clientele to raise firm value. Better knowledge of the macroeconomic conditions considered by institutional investors could give REITs an understanding of when and why institutional capital is supplied or withdrawn.

This paper starts out with the introduction of the research questions. Next, the findings from the literature on the determinants of institutional ownership are critically evaluated. In this context, our contribution to the literature is emphasized through an identification of research gaps and methodological shortcomings of past studies. This is followed by a description of the dataset to illustrate the properties of institutionally and individually owned REITs. The identification strategy is then discussed and is followed by a presentation of the estimation results. Based on our findings, a model is proposed that explains institutional ownership and provides a guide for future research on how institutional ownership is determined. The chapter concludes with a summary of the most important findings and suggests methods to overcome methodological shortcomings of past studies for future research in this field.

The final chapter of the dissertation revisits the major findings of the three papers, highlights their contribution to the literature, derives practical implications and points to further research.

2 Corporate Governance and REITs

This chapter introduces the concept of corporate governance and the associated agency theory from a general finance perspective. It then discusses what corporate governance means given the many special features of REITs and how these corporate features add to the identification strategies of the papers.

2.1 Corporate Governance and Agency Theory

This section lays the foundation for the thesis by introducing the theoretical background for the corporate governance discussion. Agency theory, in turn, substantiates the need for corporate governance and, therefore, both agency theory and corporate governance are treated jointly. Further, the economic relevance of corporate governance and associated agency conflicts are illustrated against the background of the historical development of financial markets and with special reference to recent market distortions.

Corporate governance "deals with the ways in which suppliers of finance to corporations assure themselves of getting a return on their investment" (Shleifer and Vishny, 1997, p. 737). Credible and efficient corporate governance promotes the supply of large sums of money to firms and the repatriation of returns to the financers. It reduces the cost of capital and ensures an efficient allocation of resources. Countries that lack corporate governance receive less investment from foreign investors as a result of greater information asymmetries, uncertainty and monitoring costs.[2]

The necessity for corporate governance results from the separation of ownership and control, which leads to agency conflicts and agency costs.[3] The associated agency theory is "the study of the inevitable conflicts of interest that occur when individuals engage in cooperative behavior" (Jensen, 1993, p. 870). The focus of agency theory is on the people in a company with their individual interests and incentives rather than on the firm as the sum of its assets. It deals with the costs resulting from the discrepancy between managers' and shareholders' interests that may materialize in the entrenched and self-interested decisions of the manager. Opportunistic managerial behavior in the form of perk consumption and selfish risk choices can lead to costs that impair corporate performance and shareholder wealth.

Our discussion of agency theory departs from that of Jensen and Meckling (1976) and Fama and Jensen (1983). In a principal-agent relationship the principal delegates the management duties to an agent. Their relationship is based on trust, transparency and accountability. The principal trusts the agent to diligently pursue the maximization of the principal's wealth. Transparency is achieved through fair and accurate financial reporting. To establish accountability, the agent has to justify his actions regularly and assume liability

---

[2] Leuz et al. (2010) find that foreign investors favor strong outsider protection, disclosure requirements and ownership structures that are conducive to corporate governance.

[3] In contrast to the separation of ownership and control, there are firms with a sole proprietorship that involve no conflicts of interest.

for damages arising in the case of mismanagement.

However, the actions of the agent are not always in the best interest of the principal. If the incentives of the manager and the objectives of the shareholders are at variance, agency costs may arise. The discrepancy widens as information asymmetries between principal and agent become more pronounced, which limits transparency and complicates the evaluation of managerial actions. Agency problems are not only of concern to shareholders; they also affect external stakeholders, employees, suppliers and customers (John and John, 1993). The economic significance of agency costs is discussed in many studies (e.g. Shleifer and Vishny, 1997; Gompers et al., 2003; Bebchuk et al., 2009a).

Agency theory has changed corporate finance and organizational theory. It calls for a detailed behavioral foundation of corporate decision making. The neoclassical assumption that firms maximize shareholder value is not any longer considered a valid assumption. The view that the performance of a company is solely driven by the skill, economic foresight, rationality, creative innovativeness and knowledge of customers' desires neglects a behavioral component (Morck and Yeung, 2010). The view of company decision making is now a different one: Executives may not act in the best interest of shareholders but rather in their own self-interest. Hence, corporate actions are the result of individuals pursuing own interests to maximize their utility. Firms are only maximizing shareholder wealth if the utility functions of the people in the company are consistent with the wealth maximization objective.

Company managers that demonstrate their compliance with corporate governance standards have a competitive advantage in the market. In contrast, investors will charge those firms that fail to engage in such efforts a risk premium. Firms can commit to compliance by applying well-structured compensation schemes, establishing independent boards, employing trustworthy directors and voluntarily disclosing information. Such efforts may contribute to lowering agency costs and improving the efficiency of capital allocation.

Corporate governance has only recently attracted a significant amount of attention. What factors initiated the resurgence of corporate governance? The reasons are rooted in the changing incentive structure in financial markets; the utility function of managers has changed significantly over the last 30 years. Far-reaching financial innovation and deregulation have altered the way financial markets operate. For both institutional and individual investors the markets have become more accessible, liquid and efficient, and barriers that restricted innovation and competition have been eliminated. As a result, financial markets have experienced enhanced financial engineering, portfolio optimization and securitization, amplified by technological advancements that have facilitated greater transparency and a reduction of information asymmetries. Throughout this development, managerial incentives have become increasingly performance-linked with the intent to increase shareholder wealth. Competition among firms in the financial sector has increased in tandem with deregulation. Pressure has also come from capital markets as investments have become more liquid, which has enabled investors to "vote with their feet" if they are dissatisfied with the management. To keep pace with this development the fixed portion of compensation has successively decreased while the variable portion - bonus payments - has increased. At first sight, a largely sales-volume-related compensation appears to be in accordance with shareholders' interests. While performance based compensation has motivated managers to perform better, it has also changed the nature of risks associated with an investment; managers have become more inclined to pursue aggressive risk strategies and, in rare cases, to engage in deceptive accounting practices to achieve performance targets. [4]

Although this historical development has increased managers' willingness to take on more risk, their compensation contracts have often failed to adequately consider risks relative to returns.[5] Distorted incentives can be the result: Managers benefit from the upside potential of the firm through bonuses, but do not generally participate in losses as costs of poor decisions are passed on to shareholders and creditors. This compensation structure, which is convex in returns, incentivizes managers to take on even more risk. In particular, managers have become inclined to take on tail risks, which have a severe adverse impact in improbable instances but increase returns otherwise.[6]

There are numerous mechanisms to deal with the far-reaching, mostly unobservable threat of opportunistic behavior. One way to control opportunistic

[4] Rajan (2005) critically reflects on the additional risks involved in today's financial systems and insistently stresses his concern about distorted incentives.

[5] Measuring risk is far more difficult than measuring return. The difficulty of measuring risks in today's complex financial markets becomes apparent considering recent appraisals of rating agencies. Although the measurement of risk is their core competence, rating agencies often fail at new financial products (Morgan, 2002). This materialized, for example, in overly optimistic ratings of structured asset-backed securities, which contributed to the inflation of the subprime bubble.

[6] Investments with pronounced tail risks produce low volatility but have the risk of a large loss. Taleb (2007, p. 204) gives the illustrative, yet exaggerated, example that harvesting returns of investments with great tail risks or, in his words, "black swans" is like "collecting nickels in front of steamrollers".

risk choices of managers would be to incorporate greater accountability and liability through a legal framework. The Sarbanes-Oxley Act (SOX) constitutes such a legal framework in the US and was enacted in 2002 in a response to accounting scandals, such as those of the energy company Enron in 2001 and the telecommunications company WorldCom in 2002.[7] The SOX aims at restoring confidence into corporate governance of public companies. Stricter requirements for disclosure and greater penalties for fraudulent mismanagement are intended to provide investors with greater transparency and accountability of managers' actions. The SOX requires chief executive officers (CEOs) and chief financial officers (CFOs) to personally verify financial statements and evaluate the effectiveness of internal control in the annual report. Furthermore, SOX requires management's judgment to be confirmed by external auditors. As part of SOX's greater disclosure requirements, special-purpose vehicles and off-balance-sheet transactions as well insider trades and bonuses have to be reported in greater detail. In addition, the penalties associated with fraudulent misconduct have been widened and defined more clearly.

Yet, legal structures are not sufficient to ensure that managers will act in the shareholders' interest. The SOX failed to prevent poor governance and consequent failures of the US investment banks Bear Stearns in March of 2008 and Lehman Brothers in September of 2008, with the latter triggering the financial crisis. Top

[7] Europe and Asia followed with corporate and accounting scandals of their own: the Dutch retail group Royal Ahold in 2003, the Italian food corporation Parmalat in 2003 and the China Aviation Oil in 2004. The fraudulent activities in these companies involved false accounting, deception of investors, insider trading and violation of securities law.

executives of these companies received vast amounts of performance-based compensation in the period 2000 to 2008, which encouraged them to take on excessive risk. Subprime debt was hidden off-balance sheet through Repo 105 transactions, which helped polish financial statements. During that period the compensation of Lehman's top management amounted to US $ 2.4 billion, which could not be reclaimed after the company failed (Bebchuk et al., 2009b).

Academics were the first to point out the possible threats associated with misaligned compensation schemes. Numerous studies (e.g. Morgan, 2002; Rajan, 2005) exist that should have alerted investors and supervisory authorities to exercise greater prudence in the market prior to the subprime and the financial crisis. Academic research has a role to play not only in monitoring the markets progress but also in fostering financial innovation. As part of this role it should continue its efforts to (a) identify agency conflicts, (b) point to possible consequences and (c) suggest counter measures and preventive actions for a safer development of financial markets while at the same time maintaining an unbiased and critical perspective. The academic contribution is valuable to managers, investors and policy makers as it can help them to deal with the uncertainty about incentives, understand why people act opportunistically and overcome agency conflicts via legal boundaries, appropriate incentive structures and effective monitoring.

The academic literature frames corporate governance broadly, beyond the legal framework. Corporate governance includes internal and external control mechanisms that facilitate continuous monitoring of the management, assure risk control, provide incentives for responsible management and establish an alignment of managerial incentives and shareholders' interests. The mechanisms that alleviate agency problems and promote corporate governance are subsumed under six categories that follow the definition of Brealey et al. (2008):

- Regulations and laws to protect shareholders from managerial opportunistic behavior,
- disclosure requirements and reporting standards to provide a transparent view on the company's business,
- monitoring by institutions and financial intermediaries to guard their investments,
- supervision by the board of directors,
- the threat of a takeover that presents the manager with a risk of being replaced,
- compensation structures that align the interests of shareholders with those of managers.

Market efficiency does its own part to reduce agency conflicts according to neoclassical theory. In efficient markets the founder of the firm pays most of the agency costs by issuing his shares at depressed prices, which reflect costs for monitoring and control mechanisms. Firms that do not ensure that their corporate officers will diligently handle shareholders' funds are likely to be punished by a greater stock price discount and an associated increase in the cost of capital.

However, the costs and benefits of corporate governance should find a balance. A nearly complete protection of shareholders from opportunistic actions of managers would not only be difficult to implement but would also confront shareholders with excessive costs. Empirically, it is complicated to predict and judge a manager's behavior; control mechanisms are expensive, difficult to implement and hardly accurate. Monitoring mechanisms that aim at knowing every detail of managers' actions and why they are doing it, therefore, would generate new inefficiencies, such as managerial inflexibility and excessive risk aversion. Giving managers freedom and discretion in responding to unanticipated opportunities and problems is essential for efficiency. This freedom and discretion, however, can motivate managers to act according to their self-interests to the detriment of shareholders' interests; as a result agency problems are very likely. Hence, neither overly strong nor lax corporate governance will maximize shareholder wealth (Adams et al., 2005; Adams and Ferreira, 2007). The ideal balance of corporate governance mechanisms depends on the regulations set by policy makers and the efficiency provided by capital markets.[8]

2.2 Corporate Governance in the REIT Market

The REIT market provides a unique laboratory for studying corporate governance issues. Its key features and how they are useful for the studies of corporate governance is laid out next.

[8] Strongly regulated legal frameworks and highly efficient capital markets may reduce the need for strong internal corporate governance mechanisms. In contrast, a weak legal framework with lax disclosure requirements, and inefficient capital markets with high information asymmetries may increase the need for corporate governance mechanisms.

The real estate investment trust is a tax-transparent corporate entity that invests in real estate. Its special feature is the reduction of corporate tax. In return it requires the distribution of a great portion of earnings to investors (USA: 95% prior to 2001, 90% thereafter). REITs provide a liquid structure for the illiquid real estate asset. They can be traded publicly on stock exchanges or held privately. Depending on their mix of assets they are classified as equity, hybrid or mortgage REITs. Equity REITs own real estate, mortgage REITs invest in loans secured by real estate. Hybrid REITs combine both types of investments.

This thesis focuses on publicly traded equity REITs, because they provide a fairly homogenous group of real estate investment firms that conform in terms of the dividend payout strategy, underlying asset portfolio, and organizational and corporate structure.[9] Most importantly, US equity REITs exhibit three corporate governance issues that make them particularly useful for the studies of this thesis:

First, ownership limitations due to the "five or fewer" rule limit the functionality of the market for corporate control for REITs (Ghosh and Sirmans, 2003; Eichholtz and Kok, 2008).[10] Therefore, a functioning corporate governance

[9] Real Estate Operating Companies (REOCs), which are included in the dataset of paper two, are less restricted than REITs. REOCs are flexible in their dividend payout strategy and can reinvest earnings to grow with internal funds. They are also more flexible in their operations and focus more on the development of real estate, whereas REITs rather buy, hold and sell real estate. There is tendency of REOCs to favor hotels because REITs are legally not allowed to operate or manage this type of real estate.

[10] The "five or fewer" rule (US Internal Revenue Code of 1986, Section 856(a)(6)) prevents five or fewer shareholders from holding 50 percent or more in a REIT. However, the passing of the "look-through" provision as part of the Omnibus Budget Reconciliation Act of 1993 relaxes the

structure that aligns the interests of shareholders and managers, and that assures managerial monitoring and corporate control, is of utmost importance for REITs.

Second, there are two types of advisor structures of REITs: external and internal advising. The different compensation structures between the two types make a study of the impact of managerial incentives on capital structure variation possible (chapter three). Monetary incentives of externally advised REITs that emphasize assets under management rather than income measures may encourage managers to take opportunistic action, such as excessive use of debt for corporate growth.

Third, the REIT market offers a unique laboratory for studying the performance impact of greater institutional participation (chapter four) and the drivers of institutional investment (chapter five). Institutions invest in securitized real estate for different reasons than they do in other markets. Hence, the drivers of institutional investment identified in the finance literature may not apply to the REIT market. The role of institutional investors with respect to corporate governance is not clear either. Although mechanisms for corporate control, such as minimum dividend payout and transparent reporting, are present in the REIT market, institutional investors may still play an important role in alleviating agency conflicts and, thereby, increasing market and operating performance.

The US equity REIT market offers a long time series and a large cross-section

restrictions of the "five or fewer" rule for pension funds. This makes it possible for pension funds to accumulate a larger stake in a REIT, which gives them greater say and monitoring power.

for our datasets. Although REIT markets around the world are growing rapidly, only the US market provides unmatched data quality, which makes it possible to apply robust panel models with firm fixed-effects to allow for causal inference. It is the largest in terms of market capitalization and efficiency. SNL Financial and the Center for Research in Security Prices (CRSP) provide the datasets of this thesis with up to 265 firms for a time series from 1994 until 2010.[11]

[11] The datasets of chapter four and chapter five cover fewer firms since they work with additional data on institutional ownership for which availability is limited. Chapter four also includes REOCs in order to draw inferences on a broader market for indirect real estate investments.

3 Corporate Governance and the Leverage of REITs: The Impact of the Advisor Structure

This chapter is based on Striewe, N. C., Rottke, N. B., and Zietz, J. (2013). Corporate Governance and the Leverage of REITs: The Impact of the Advisor Structure. *Journal of Real Estate Research*, Vol. 35, No. 1, pp. 103-119.

Acknowledgements: We thank our colleague John Glascock as well as the participants of the 16th ERES Conference in Stockholm and the 26th ARES Conference in Naples for their comments on earlier versions of this paper. We also gratefully acknowledge the many helpful comments of the referees, without implicating them for any remaining errors.

3 Corporate Governance and the Leverage of REITs: The Impact of the Advisor Structure

3.1 Introduction

The purpose of this paper is to investigate an important corporate governance issue: How does the advisor structure affect the leverage of real estate investment trusts (REITs). Advisors are expected to pursue personal goals, such as the maximization of their compensation and personal assets. If these personal goals of the advisors are not aligned with shareholder wealth maximization, agency conflicts may arise. Observing how the capital structure varies in conjunction with the advisor structure can identify such agency conflicts.

The potential for agency conflicts in the external advisor structure of REITs has been highlighted by Finnerty and Park (1991) and Capozza and Seguin (2000, hereafter C&S). C&S go one step further and suggest that there is empirical evidence for this agency conflict. They find that externally advised REITs choose higher leverage than internally advised REITs. C&S interpret this as a serious conflict between the interests of shareholders and external REIT advisors. They suggest that the excessive leverage may be attributable to a misaligned compensation scheme of external advisors that neglects interest expenses.

C&S's study period from 1985 to 1992 is characterized by a wave of externally advised REITs converting to the internally advised and internally managed form. A change in the regulation in 1986 first allowed REITs to operate and manage properties themselves. Ott et al. (2005) describe the early REIT years from 1981 to 1992 as the old REIT era, populated with "sleepy, slow-growth" companies; the authors characterize the "dynamic, high-growth" period from 1993 onward as the new REIT era. In the old REIT era, which includes the period of the changing governance structure analyzed by C&S, externally advised REITs attracted considerable attention for their agency issues and underperformance. To escape this controversy, many externally advised REITs converted to an internally advised and internally managed structure starting in 1986. REITs also changed with respect to operating characteristics in the new REIT era: One finds greater transparency, stabilized financing, higher institutional ownership, more complex capital structures and greater internal growth. Along similar lines, Ambrose and Linneman (2001) identify a convergence of operating characteristics of externally and internally advised REITs in the new REIT era. The REIT modernization act of 1999 brought about further structural changes affecting the way REITs are operated and financed.[12] As a consequence, agency conflicts in externally advised REITs should be less evident in more recent data.

We focus our study on the impact of the advisor structure on leverage for the

---

[12] The REIT Modernization Act of 1999 became effective in 2001. It has reduced the payout ratio from 95% to 90% and has introduced the Taxable REIT Subsidiary. Both regulatory changes have had a significant impact on REITs, giving managers twice the amount of cash flow to work with and allowing them to expand their activities by providing services to tenants and others.

new REIT era, that is, for the period that follows the conversion of the majority of externally advised REITs to internally advised ones. Our study uses data on US equity REITs from 1994 to 2010 to test whether the charges brought upon externally advised REITs regarding agency issues during the old REIT era still exist today in the new REIT era. Our expectation is that the more sophisticated environment of the new REIT era monitors the behavior of external advisors more effectively and, therefore, drives external advisors to make competitive and prudent investment decisions with less opportunistic motivation.

We find that externally advised REITs choose lower leverage levels than their internally advised counterparts for the new REIT era. This makes economic sense considering the fact that externally advised REITs bear higher cost of debt. Hence, there is no reason to suspect an agency problem for externally advised REITs in the new REIT era.

The remainder of the paper is organized as follows. Section two gives an overview of the relevant theories on capital structure as they relate to corporate governance and associated empirical findings. Section three describes the dataset and discusses the empirical methodology. Section four presents the estimation results. Section five concludes with a summary of the study's most important results.

3.2 Theoretical Background

3.2.1 Capital Structure Theories

The following section reviews and discusses the capital structure theories from the finance literature. They lay out the theoretical fundament for the paper, which studies agency conflicts visible in capital structure variation of REITs. We consider the trade-off theory, the pecking order theory and the market timing theory as controls in explaining leverage to isolate the impact of the advisor structure.

Capital structure theories analyze the relationship between corporate capital structure decisions and the market value of the firm. Early on, Modigliani and Miller (1958) asserted that there exists no relationship between a firm's value and its capital structure. This view rests on efficient market assumptions, that there are no tax benefits of debt, that interest rates are the same for the corporation and the investor, and that no information gap exists between them. Furthermore, the absence of transactions costs and any costs of financial distress is assumed.

The evolution of capital structure theory is closely tied to relaxing the controversial assumptions of Modigliani and Miller (1958). For example, by considering the tax benefits of debt, Modigliani and Miller (1963) find that increasing debt levels are related to an increasing firm value. This effect is partly compensated for by personal taxes according to Miller (1977).

Allowing for costs of bankruptcy and certain types of tax-shields (DeAngelo and Masulis, 1980) results in the *trade-off theory* in which there is an optimal capital structure. At the optimal level, the benefits and costs of debt are balanced. The benefits of debt are mainly the tax deductibility of interest payments and the signaling characteristic of debt for high company performance. The costs of debt include higher risk of bankruptcy. Altman (1984) finds that bankrupt companies are mostly overleveraged and the expected costs of bankruptcy are higher than the present value of the tax benefits. According to the static trade-off theory, a company adjusts equity and debt until a certain optimum is found that maximizes firm value.

The *pecking order theory* was developed as a way to incorporate information asymmetries between the manager and the investor into a model of capital structure. It implies that there is no optimal leverage but rather a preference ordering of financing sources (Myers, 1984; Myers and Majluf, 1984). The pecking order theory predicts that managers prefer internal over external financing. If external financing is necessary, the manager is expected to start with debt, then hybrid financing; equity financing is a last resort. This can lead to a problematic reaction of investors in case of an equity issue. Investors may interpret the issuing of equity as a signal that the manager regards the company value as too high.[13] Investors may react by selling shares. This idea was first raised when Donaldson (1961) conducted a study on large companies and discovered the preference pattern for financing sources. Empirically the pecking order theory shows greater

[13] An equity issue when the share price of the company is overvalued may be attractive for the company as the share price is expected to adjust downward to a more appropriate level in the future.

validity in companies with higher agency costs (Leary and Roberts, 2010). The pecking order theory manifests in a firm's preference for higher leverage at start-up[14] when negative cash flows are more likely, information asymmetry is higher, and an equity issue is, therefore, unattractive.

Fama and French (2005) suggest that the applicability of the pecking order theory to capital structure decisions is limited. An assumption of the pecking order is that an equity issue is necessarily associated with asymmetric information. This disregards the possibility that there may be ways to avoid asymmetric information. Also Barclay and Smith (2005) provide empirical evidence contrary to the predictions of the pecking order theory. They show that profitable companies choose above-average leverage and start-up firms tend to be mostly financed with equity.

Market timing, a third theory for capital structure that is experiencing new popularity, stems from the work of Myers (1984): Capital structure decisions hinge on market factors. The theory is that managers choose debt or equity as a function of the respective market environment. Market timing behavior is the effort of firms to time the market to reduce their cost of capital (Baker and Wurgler, 2002). Managers are inclined to issue equity when they perceive the stock price to be high and prefer debt financing in times of undervaluation. If both equity and debt markets fail to offer attractive conditions, managers tend to defer external financing and rather source from internal funds. Vice versa, in the

---

[14] Start-up companies are usually characterized by high growth opportunities.

presence of attractive market conditions managers may feel urged to excessively draw funds from both equity and debt markets regardless of an immediate use. Therefore, market timing behavior is essential to consider in models that explain capital structure variation over time. A capital structure model should use proxies for debt market and equity market conditions to measure market timing effects or, alternatively, include time fixed-effects as controls.

Newer studies weaken the explanatory power of the presented capital structure theories. Lemmon et al. (2008) find that capital structures are persistent and are primarily driven by time-invariant fixed-effects. Apparently, unobserved firm characteristics are of first order importance in explaining variations in capital structure in the cross-section.

3.2.2 Capital Structure of REITs

Capital structure theories have been designed and tested primarily on non-property companies.[15] REITs, however, exhibit characteristics that may limit the applicability of the theories. Their characteristics of interest for capital structure theory and associated implications are outlined in this section.

First, the costs of bankruptcy are rather low for REITs compared to non-property companies, although they cannot be fully neglected. REITs and property companies have on average a higher debt capacity in comparison to non-property

[15] Most studies on capital structure exclude financial, insurance and real estate firms (SIC codes 6000-6900) as well as regulated industries (SIC codes 4900-4999) from the sample (Fama and French, 2002; Leary and Roberts, 2005; Flannery and Rangan, 2006; Chang and Dasgupta, 2009).

companies (Chan et al., 2003) due to the high volume invested in property. The tangibility of real estate assets, which can usually be sold in the market at a small discount, generally leads to higher collateral values. Lenders may have more trust in a company's ability to recover from financial difficulty if many marketable real estate assets are in the company's portfolio and cash-flows are steady in the long run.[16] However, this specific focus on an asset class entails a limitation to diversify; REITs are usually focused locally and on one property type. The resulting high sensitivity to cyclicalities of their respective investments can magnify bankruptcy costs and decrease the potential debt capacity.

Second, the special tax status of REITs also weakens the applicability of the trade-off theory. The assumption of tax deductibility in the static trade-off theory does not hold true for REITs because their distributed income is tax-exempt[17] and, therefore, a benefit from the tax-shield is non-existent.

Third, the limited ability to build up reserves from internally generated funds should strongly influence capital structure decisions and it may counteract many of the effects predicted by the pecking order theory for REITs. The majority of earnings have to be distributed to the shareholders and are not at the disposal of the manager.

Fourth, REITs should be less impacted by the free cash flow problem, because

---

[16] In crises of the housing sector lenders may perceive real estate assets as a hazard as well.

[17] Only the income that is distributed to investors is tax-exempt. REITs in the US have to distribute at least 90 percent of their income. The income not distributed is subject to corporate income tax.

REITs are required to distribute at least 90 percent of their earnings to shareholders, which leaves less free cash flow at the disposal of the manager. Consequently, REITs have to approach external financing sources anew each time a project is initiated, requiring managers to justify their actions more frequently and exposing them to greater monitoring. Jensen (1989) describes the conflict between principal and agent over the use of free cash flows as the "central source of waste" in a publicly held company. Inside financing with retained earnings is convenient for the manager as it means minimum effort and justification. Outside financing, in contrast, involves monitoring of the management because raising funds from external sources involves a detailed reporting of the new funds' allocation. In accordance, agency theory predicts that internal funds (free cash-flows) are allocated less efficiently and their allocation is affected by greater opportunistic motivation.

3.2.3 Corporate Governance and Capital Structure

Corporate governance is associated with capital structure variation. Research on corporate governance began with Jensen and Meckling (1976). The key issue of corporate governance is to identify ways to reduce the potential for opportunistic behavior on the part of the manager.

There are four basic types of agency conflicts that are relevant to the advisor structure: (1) the desire of managers to remain in power, (2) to maximize compensation and personal assets, (3) to concentrate his/her control over the company, and (4) to avoid managerial risk. First, managers may act opportunistically to retain their jobs even though a replacement of the management team may maximize shareholder value in certain circumstances. Second, the manager may be driven by the desire to maximize compensation while making corporate decisions. Third, the director may have an incentive to adjust the capital structure to increase his/her control over the company. Last but not least, while typical shareholders hold diversified portfolios, managers are likely to bear cluster risks because a large part of their personal portfolios is invested in their company and their human capital is tied to the company (Fama, 1980). This higher risk exposure can let managers avoid projects that may be attractive to shareholders from a net present value perspective but are a threat from a manager's point of view. Managerial risk aversion may also cause opportunistic behavior on capital structure decisions, as the risks associated with debt may impact compensation and control.

These agency issues become a problem when information asymmetries are pronounced. In the REIT market information asymmetries should be quite large. REITs are typically small firms with lower trading volumes relative to common stock companies (Glascock et al., 1998). Liquidity is lower in the REIT market (Below et al., 1995), institutional ownership increased only recently and fewer analysts cover REITs (Wang et al., 1995a; Su Han et al., 1998). The appraisal of properties and its public announcement leads to a temporary information gap in which insiders know the appraisal value while outsiders do not (Damodaran et al., 1993). These particularities are associated with reduced information disclosure, and private information in this case might create adverse-selection problems.[18]

Table 1: Number of REITs by Management and Advisor Structure

	Externally Advised	Internally Advised
Externally Managed	26	42
Internally Managed	3	194

Notes: The data cover 265 publicly traded US REITs from 1994Q1 to 2010Q4

REITs are either internally or externally advised. A REIT is externally advised if asset management services (investment/disposition decisions) are provided by a separate company that is not a subsidiary.[19] The majority of today's REITs is internally advised and internally managed (Table 1). Most REITs that choose to be externally advised also hire external property managers.

The passage of the Tax Reform Act of 1986 that, for the first time, allowed REITs to operate and self-manage properties paved the way for REITs to become fully integrated (internally advised and internally managed). Prior to 1986, REITs were exclusively externally managed by law.

Externally advised REITs provide certain benefits: External advisors can manage multiple REITs at economical costs and usually have high skills and a

[18] REITs also offer some transparency advantages. The cash flow of REITs is usually steady, income statements are mostly transparent, and items like R&D expenditures tend to be low. Also, benchmark prices on the parallel real estate market are available for comparison and uncertainty has been reduced in general (Below et al., 1996). These transparency advantages ease the access to equity markets for REITs.

[19] REITs also choose to be internally or externally managed; they either manage day-to-day operations of properties themselves or engage external property managers. Property managers are not directly involved in financing activities and should not impact capital structure decisions. Our definitions of "advised" and "managed" follow those of Ambrose and Linneman (2001) and SNL Financial.

pool of qualified employees that they can access. In particular, smaller REITs could be managed cost-efficiently by external advisors because they benefit from scale economies compared to a dedicated internal management team.

Compelling evidence about agency conflicts inherent in externally advised REITs clouds the benefits of external advising. Decision makers of internally advised REITs face performance incentives that are determined by net income at the corporate level. Thus, they pay attention to interest expenses in their decision-making. Advisors of externally advised REITs are usually compensated according to assets under management and property-level cash flows. This may provide an incentive to increase the asset base under management (Jenkins, 1980; Sagalyn, 1996). External advisors may, therefore, be tempted to raise leverage more than is consistent with shareholder wealth maximization because interest expenses are not impacting their compensation. For the same reason external advisors may have less incentive to negotiate for attractive interest rates. Additional external advisor fees apply for property acquisitions, increasing the incentive for excessive expansion even further.

The potential for such opportunistic behavior may become a threat if corporate control mechanisms are weak. The old REIT era, prior to 1993, is characterized by weak corporate control mechanisms, such as little analyst coverage and low institutional ownership. Studying the time period from 1985 to 1992, which covers the years when many REITs switched from an external to an internal advising mode, C&S find empirical evidence for opportunistic behavior: Their study shows that externally advised REITs have higher leverage levels than their internally advised counterparts.

3.2.4 Control Variables and Dependent Variable

Managers of growing companies tend to prefer maximum control over their decisions. Debt can negatively affect their freedom to make decisions in case of financial distress. That is more likely a problem for growing companies as they have more volatile earnings. However, the causation may also operate in the opposite direction. Debt avoids growing firms because creditors try to avoid the problems associated with higher information asymmetry, agency cost, and risk of bankruptcy. The market-to-book ratio is the most commonly used and the most reliable proxy for *growth opportunities* (Frank and Goyal, 2009). The market-to-book ratio is also a proxy for the market valuation of the firm. This means that market timing behavior is measured in tandem with the effects of growth opportunities.

The pecking order theory suggests a negative impact of firm *size* on leverage. Information asymmetries decline as the company gets larger because more information is disclosed to shareholders. Hence, large firms enjoy lower costs for issuing equity and, therefore, choose less debt. The trade-off theory predicts larger REITs to have more debt since they tend to be more diversified and bear lower bankruptcy risk. Firm size is approximated by the natural logarithm of total assets, deflated by the US consumer price index (CPI). The logarithmic transformation allows for a possible nonlinear impact of firm size.

The prediction of the trade-off theory is a positive relationship between the degree of *asset tangibility* and leverage. A company has a better chance to recover from financial difficulty and meet debt service when its assets are highly tangible.[20] Our model uses real estate investments as a percentage of total assets as a proxy.[21]

Profitable companies generate more internal funds to finance new projects (pecking order theory). As a consequence, there is less need to resort to external financing.[22] A profitable firm, therefore, is expected to decrease leverage because future investments are financed internally and debt is paid back.[23] *Profitability* is approximated by return on assets.

Companies with volatile earnings are at greater risk of bankruptcy because earnings are more likely to drop below debt service commitments. The pecking order theory proposes that firms with volatile earnings suffer from adverse selection limiting the access to capital markets. Hence, debt may be the preferred choice. This effect is captured by the control variable *earnings volatility*.[24]

The *dividend payout* ratio should be negatively related to leverage (Frank and Goyal, 2009). For REITs, there is less variation in the dividend payout levels

---

[20] The pecking order theory predicts a negative impact of asset tangibility on leverage. It rests on the idea that companies with lower asset tangibility have higher information asymmetries. A larger mispricing of equity is the result and debt is preferred.

[21] A REIT must invest at least 75% of its assets in real estate, cash and cash items (including receivables) and government securities (US Internal Revenue Code § 856(c)(4)(A): "75 Percent Asset Test").

[22] This point should be less relevant for REITs because the distribution requirement of 90 percent on earnings limits their ability to build up reserves.

[23] The trade-off theory suggests the inverse relationship, based on the assumption that the benefit from the tax-shield of debt increases with higher profitability. This view predicts that higher profitability of taxable companies coincides with higher leverage. The trade-off theory is far less valid for REITs due to their special tax status.

[24] The standard deviation of excess returns in lieu of earnings volatility is used as a robustness check. Our results do not materially change.

because the lower boundary for earnings payout is fixed at 90% (95% prior to 2001). We use the ratio of dividends to funds from operations as the proxy for *dividend payout*.

Firms do not rebalance stock market induced changes in their capital structure (Welch, 2004). Hence, stock price changes move leverage away from desired targets. Stock market conditions not only passively impact the capital structure but also drive managers to exploit market timing (Baker and Wurgler, 2002). Managers actively time markets to benefit from mispricing. We control for these effects by including the change in stock price (*stock performance*) in our models.

Ooi et al. (2010) test the influence that market conditions have on financing decisions of REITs. The authors find that REITs consider capital market conditions to time their financing. We use time fixed-effects to account for time-varying unobserved effects that impact all REITs.

Leverage can be measured in various ways. Even though most predictions apply directly to book values, there is still dissent on the appropriate proxy for leverage. We use both *book leverage* and *market leverage* as dependent variables. *Book leverage* reflects events from the past, whereas *market leverage* is forward-looking and is suited to capture effects from market factors (Frank and Goyal, 2009). Accounting for the criticism of Welch (2007), we calculate *book leverage* by dividing financial debt by the sum of the book value of equity and financial debt. We define *market leverage* as financial debt divided by the sum of the market value of equity and financial debt.[25]

3.3 Data and Methodology

The data cover 265 publicly listed US equity REITs (Table 2). We avoid a survivorship bias[26] by including defunct entities that do not exist as separate entities up to the end of the sample because of mergers or acquisitions or that join the sample after 1994 because of a later initial public offering (IPO). Financial data are derived from the SNL Financial database and stock price data from the Center for Research in Security Prices (CRSP). Our models use quarterly observations from 1994Q1 to 2010Q4.[27]

Our identification strategy to measure the impact of advisor structure on leverage makes use of a property type fixed-effects estimator.[28] Controlling for property type fixed-effects is crucial in our study because externally advised REITs tend to invest in different property types than their internally advised

[25] We also estimate our models with the debt ratios that include non-financial liabilities, which are for book leverage [1- book value of equity / book value of assets] and for market leverage [1- market value of equity / (market value of equity + book value of liabilities)]. This alternative specification does not materially change our results.

[26] Survivors tend to be larger and more profitable. They have fewer growth opportunities, higher levels of asset tangibility and higher levels of leverage (Lemmon et al., 2008).

[27] SNL Financial provides only scarce data on externally advised REITs for the periods prior to 1994Q1. The database extended REIT coverage starting 1994Q1 for all our model components.

[28] The pooled model is tested against the random effects model via the Breusch-Pagan test. The test confirms, at better than the one percent level, that the simple pooled regression is rejected relative to the random effects model. The random effects model, in turn, is tested against the fixed-effects model via the Hausman test. The random effects model is rejected in favor of the fixed-effects model. We note that a standard firm fixed-effects model could not identify the impact of the advisor structure as it does not vary over time for a given firm.

counterparts. In particular, out of 29 externally advised REITs eight are focused on self-storage real estate and seven are diversified. None of the externally advised REITs is focused on specialty real estate (Table 2). Property type fixed-effects will account for any unobserved heterogeneity among the different property types.

Table 2: Property Focus of Externally and Internally Advised REITs

	Internally Advised			Externally Advised		
Property Focus	No.	Mean Market Leverage	Mean Book Leverage	No.	Mean Market Leverage	Mean Book Leverage
Diversified	16	40%	50%	7	47%	50%
Health Care	13	40%	49%	3	23%	29%
Hotel	21	50%	51%	1	29%	31%
Industrial	19	48%	54%	1	56%	55%
Office	37	47%	54%	4	31%	30%
Residential	46	49%	60%	1	74%	60%
Retail	63	49%	61%	4	51%	71%
Self-Storage	9	23%	29%	8	1%	2%
Specialty	12	46%	55%	0		
Total	236	46%	56%	29	27%	33%

Notes: The data cover 265 publicly traded US REITs from 1994Q1 to 2010Q4.

In our regressions we account for a number of firm-specific differences that may affect leverage outside of the type of advisor structure. In particular, we control for *growth opportunities*, *profitability*, *size*, *asset tangibility*, *earnings volatility*, *dividend payout* and *stock performance*. The definitions and basic statistics are given in Table 3. All independent variables are lagged by one period to avoid endogeneity issues. The reported standard errors are heteroscedasticity and autocorrelation consistent as suggested for datasets with a large number of cross-section units and a small number of time periods (Cameron and Trivedi, 2005). Apart from firm specific influences, leverage values may also be reacting to macroeconomic changes over time, such as variations in interest rates, the ups and downs of the business cycle, or economic crises as the one that followed the subprime-lending problem. We account for the impact of these changes in the economic environment by including time fixed-effects in all our models.

Table 3: Variable Definitions and Basic Statistics

Variable	Description	Mean	SD	Min	Max
Market leverage	Financial debt / (market value of equity + financial debt)	0.452	0.186	0.000	0.932
Book leverage	Financial debt / (book value of equity + financial debt)	0.540	0.203	0.000	1.000
Growth opportunities	Market value of equity / book value of equity	1.503	1.085	0.000	8.211
Size	Natural logarithm of total assets deflated by the US CPI.	13.737	1.362	8.565	17.205
Asset tangibility	Property investment / total assets	0.840	0.126	0.000	0.982
Profitability	Net income / total assets	0.009	0.009	-0.051	0.052
Earnings volatility	Percentage change in net income	0.006	0.297	-1.970	22.797
Dividend payout	Dividends / funds from operations	0.728	0.283	0.000	1.990
Stock performance	Change in raw stock price	0.018	0.161	-0.915	3.531

Notes: 7840 observations are available for each variable. The ratios *book leverage, market leverage, growth opportunities, asset tangibility* and *profitability* are winsorized at the 1st and the 99th percentile. The data cover 265 publicly traded US REITs from 1994Q1 to 2010Q4.

Lastly, we include an interaction term between a time trend variable and the focus variable *externally advised.* The variable *trend* is zero until 1996Q2, counts from one to two for the quarters from 1996Q3 to 1996Q4 and is constant at two thereafter.[29] It is meant to reflect the fact that the leverage levels of both advisor structures converge especially in 1996Q3 and 1996Q4, and stay at a similar rate thereafter.

3.4 Estimation Results

External advisor arrangements are negatively related to leverage for the time period from 1994 to 2010.[30] The negative relationship between leverage and the variable *externally advised* identified in Table 4 makes perfect economic sense considering the fact that externally advised REITs bear in general a higher cost of debt than internally advised REITs (Figure 1). These higher interest costs translate into a lower optimal leverage. Hence, a compensation style based on asset size does not lead to opportunistic behavior on the part of managers, and does not result in a possible disadvantage to shareholders in the new REIT era.

We also identify a converging trend of leverage between externally and internally advised entities. The coefficient of the interaction variable *trend*externally advised* shows that in 1996Q3 and 1996Q4 the leverage ratios of

---

[29] The time window is identified by an iterative procedure that tests all possible time windows in which we suspect a possible trend. The time window with the highest significance is that from 1996Q3 to 1996Q4.

[30] As a sensitivity check we compare externally advised REITs with fully integrated REITs that are both internally advised and internally managed. We also test the sensitivity of our models to a different specification of our time window that excludes the volatile quarters during the financial crisis. Our results do not materially change for these specifications.

externally and internally advised REITs converge. This indicates that during this period external advisors engaged in significant efforts to adjust their leverage closer to the levels of internally advised REITs.

Table 4: Impact of Advisor Structure on Leverage

Variable	Market Leverage			Book Leverage		
	Base	With controls	With trend	Base	With controls	With trend
Externally advised	-0.125***	-0.106***	-0.171***	-0.133***	-0.127***	-0.183***
	(0.000)	(0.000)	(0.000)	(0.001)	(0.000)	(0.000)
Trend*externally advised			0.041*			0.035
			(0.073)			(0.160)
Growth opportunities		-0.017***	-0.018***		0.048***	0.047***
		(0.009)	(0.008)		(0.000)	(0.000)
Size		-0.014**	-0.014**		-0.004	-0.004
		(0.017)	(0.014)		(0.554)	(0.519)
Asset tangibility		0.120	0.123*		0.155*	0.158*
		(0.102)	(0.093)		(0.081)	(0.076)
Profitability		-8.541***	-8.527***		-7.815***	-7.803***
		(0.000)	(0.000)		(0.000)	(0.000)
Earnings volatility		0.022***	0.022***		0.019***	0.019***
		(0.000)	(0.000)		(0.000)	(0.000)
Dividend payout		-0.049**	-0.049**		-0.021	-0.021
		(0.016)	(0.015)		(0.334)	(0.328)
Stock performance		-0.080***	-0.079***		-0.034***	-0.034***
		(0.000)	(0.000)		(0.005)	(0.005)
Constant	0.268***	0.518***	0.522***	0.424***	0.349**	0.354**
	(0.000)	(0.000)	(0.000)	(0.005)	(0.035)	(0.033)
Akaike's Information Criterion	-7343.0	-9888.5	-9913.4	-6644.0	-8700.6	-8715.6
Adjusted R^2	0.327	0.514	0.516	0.379	0.523	0.524

Notes: The table presents panel regression coefficients and the associated p-values in parentheses using property type fixed-effects and time fixed-effects. 265 REITs are included for quarterly periods from 1994Q1 to 2010Q4 (7840 observations). *Trend* is zero until 1996Q2, counts from one to two for the period 1996Q3 to 1996Q4 and is constant two thereafter. The dependent variables are *market leverage* and *book leverage*. All independent variables are lagged by one period. Standard errors are heteroscedasticity and autocorrelation consistent. * indicates significance at the 10% level, ** indicates significance at the 5% level, *** indicates significance at the 1% level.

Figure 1: Cost of Debt of Internally Advised vs. Externally Advised REITs

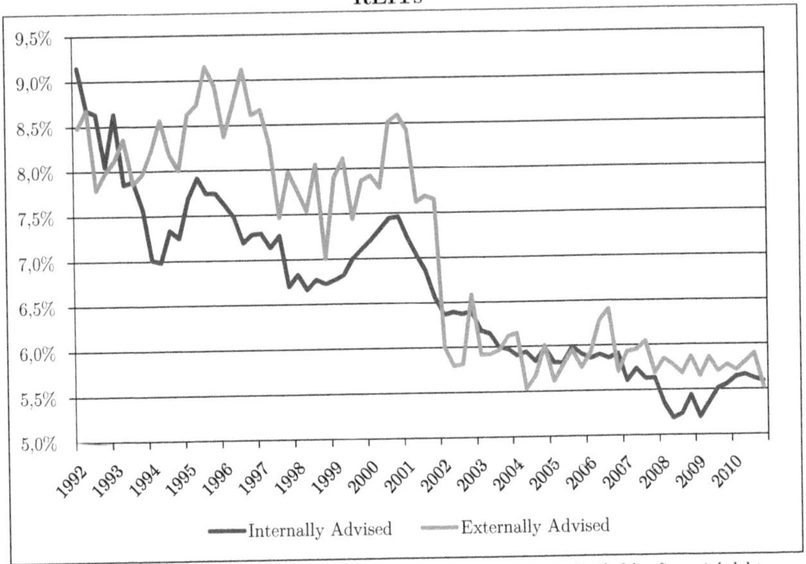

Notes: Cost of debt is defined as annualized quarterly interest expenses divided by financial debt.

The above results deviate from those of C&S, who investigate data from 1985 to 1992. External REIT advisors took advantage of their ability to increase compensation through debt increases in the old REIT era. This behavior is not found in the newer data.[31] The environment of REITs has changed in the sense that greater transparency and analyst coverage, higher institutional ownership, and greater liquidity have reduced agency issues and information asymmetries (Ott et al., 2005).

The change in behavior is likely fostered by the discussion of moral hazard issues of externally advised REITs that pressured externally advised REITs to

[31] Due to limited data availability, we are unable to run structural break tests prior to 1994Q1.

fundamentally change their behavior or convert to the internal advisor structure. Some of the pressure may also have originated from the fact that externally advised REITs experienced underperformance during the old REIT era (Howe and Shilling, 1990; Cannon and Vogt, 1995).[32]

For the early years of our study period we find that the average leverage of externally advised REITs has its lowest point. From that time onward, the leverage of externally advised REITs starts to converge upward to the much higher level of internally advised REITs (Figure 2). The market-to-book values also converge during that period, indicating that investors perceived the change of externally advised REITs positively (Figure 3).

Figure 2: Development of Leverage of US REITs

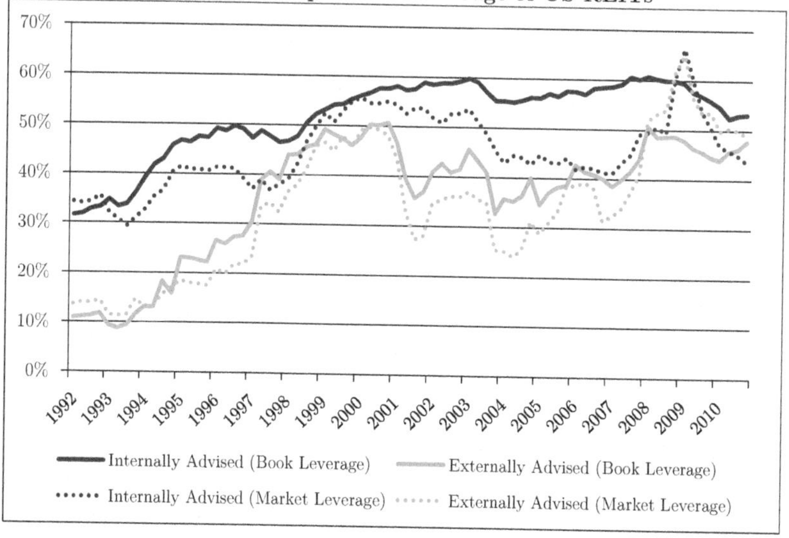

[32] Externally advised REITs are also perceived to take less advantage of economies of scale (Bers and Springer, 1997).

Figure 3: Market-to-Book Ratios of US REITs

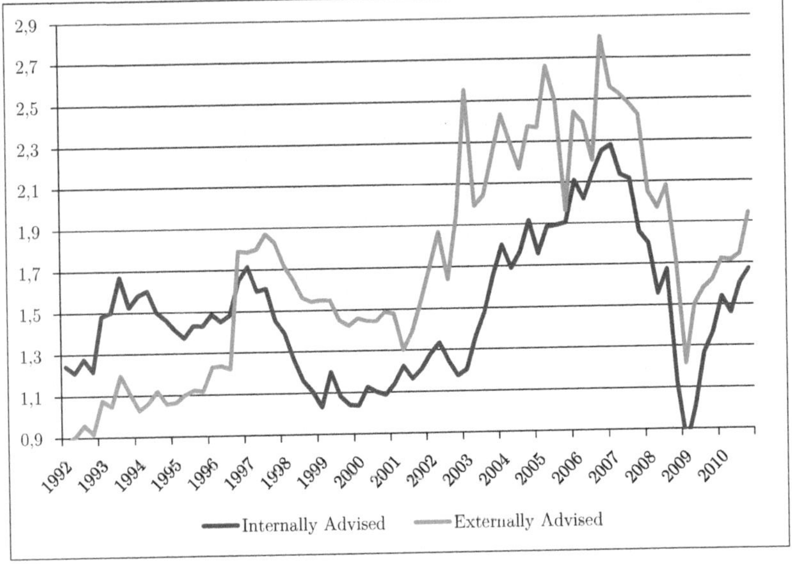

The coefficients of our control variables turn out as expected and are consistent with recent findings from Harrison et al. (2011) and Ghosh et al. (2011). *Profitability, dividend payout, size* and *stock performance* are inversely related to leverage. *Earnings volatility* and *asset tangibility* are positively related to leverage. The impact of *growth opportunities* on *book leverage* is positive and on *market leverage* negative. Time fixed-effects and property type fixed-effects are jointly significant. The interpretation of these relationships is discussed next.

The prediction of the market timing theory is supported by our findings for *growth opportunities* and *stock performance*. In particular, managers actively time the market to take advantage of mispricing (Baker and Wurgler, 2002). This finding is also consistent with the argument of Welch (2004) that firms do not rebalance stock price induced leverage variation.

The coefficient signs of *profitability, size, growth opportunities* and *earnings volatility* support the pecking order theory. This means that (a) profitable REITs become less levered over time as profits may be used to redeem debt, (b) large REITs have less information asymmetries between insiders and investors, making access to equity markets easier, (c) growing REITs with more investments accumulate more debt and, (d) volatile REITs suffer from adverse selection and, therefore, access equity markets less.

The only evidence for the impact of the trade-off theory comes from the coefficient sign of the variable *asset tangibility*. Highly tangible assets are easier to value for outsiders. The tangibility of real estate assets generally leads to higher collateral values, which can usually be sold in the market at a small discount. Accordingly, lenders have more trust in a company's ability to recover from financial difficulty if many marketable real estate assets are in the company's portfolio. Contrary to the predictions of the trade-off and the pecking order theory, higher *dividend payout* is associated with lower leverage.[33]

In summary, the market timing theory, the pecking order theory, and property type effects are important drivers of REIT leverage. The evidence for the trade-off theory is less clear. Its assumption of tax deductibility does not hold for REITs because their distributed income is tax-exempt.[34] This, in combination with a

---

[33] This finding is consistent with those of Frank and Goyal (2009) and Harrison et al. (2011). The negative relationship between dividend payout and leverage is still a puzzle in the literature and the theoretical interpretation of this issue requires further development.

[34] Only the income that is distributed to investors is tax-exempt. US REITs have to distribute at least 90 percent of their income. The income not distributed is subject to corporate income tax.

lower cost of financial distress of REITs, explains the limited applicability of the trade-off theory.

3.5 Concluding Remarks

The purpose of this paper has been to examine whether externally advised REITs have higher leverage levels than internally advised REITs, as previously reported in the literature for the old REIT era (1985-1992). We find new results for the impact of external advisors on leverage for the new REIT era.

In particular, the compensation style of externally advised REITs does not appear to lead to opportunistic behavior on the part of managers anymore; externally advised REITs do not have a perceptively higher leverage level than internally advised REITs over the period 1994 to 2010 as opposed to the period 1985 to 1992. We find that externally advised REITs choose lower leverage levels compared to their internally advised counterparts. This appears to be consistent with optimal choice behavior insofar as externally advised REITs bear higher cost of debt.

For the old REIT era, externally advised REITs are charged with agency conflicts and associated underperformance. The potential for opportunistic behavior arose from misaligned compensation schemes. As a consequence, a wave of externally advised REITs converted to being internally advised. The majority of the conversions took place in the years following the Tax Reform Act of 1986 that allowed REITs to operate and self-manage properties. According to our findings, REITs that remain externally advised in the new REIT era do not take advantage of excessive leverage anymore. The fact that some REITs decide to continue to operate with the external advisor structure is evidence that agency issues have been resolved to a large extent and some investors appreciate the benefits that externally advised REITs can have, such as scale effects, due to advisors managing multiple REITs, and access to a large pool of qualified employees.

4 The Impact of Institutional Ownership on the Performance of REITs and REOCs: The Corporate Governance Effect

This chapter is based on Striewe, N. C., Rottke, N. B. and Zietz, J. (2013). The Impact of Institutional Ownership on REIT Performance, *Journal of Real Estate Portfolio Management*, Vol. 19, No. 1, pp. 17-30.

4 The Impact of Institutional Ownership on the Performance of REITs and REOCs: The Corporate Governance Effect

4.1 Introduction

The purpose of this paper is to identify the performance impact of institutional investment for real estate investment trusts (REITs) and real estate operating companies (REOCs). The paper answers the following questions on which evidence is still inconclusive in the literature: "Is a positive change in institutional ownership associated with a persistently higher market valuation and operating performance?", "Do positive changes in institutional ownership lead to abnormal returns on the event date?" and "Do firms with agency issues benefit more from the presence of institutional investors?"

REITs and REOCs offer a fairly homogenous group of firms with a higher potential for agency issues compared to industrial firms. To alleviate agency issues, such as opportunistic managerial behavior institutions can serve as a monitoring mechanism that results in improved corporate governance (Carleton et al., 1998). Hence, higher institutional ownership may be desirable from a corporate governance perspective and may positively impact operating and market performance. Our key expectation is that, over time, higher alpha returns should not be associated with the level of institutional ownership but only with changes in it. This is because a constant level of institutional ownership does not lead to changes in expectations about the company. A corporate governance effect should be observable only when there is a change in institutional ownership. Market participants adjust their expectations about the stock price on the event date when new information is released. Hence, only a change in institutional ownership should impact risk-adjusted performance on the event date.

Wang et al. (1995b) find that firms with higher institutional ownership outperform the market. The authors measure performance with market-adjusted returns, excess returns, Jensen alpha and Sharpe ratios for the period 1970-1989. A continuously higher risk-adjusted return of institutionally owned REITs found in the study could be related to some neglected risk factor. Applying the Fama French factors augmented by an additional momentum factor can eliminate this problem. According to Cready (1994), Below et al. (2000a) and Below et al. (2000b), institutional investors have a preference for companies of a certain size, with a particular book-to-market ratio or past returns. Accordingly, measuring performance by a one-factor model could be biased because it fails to account for size and book-to-market effects as pointed out by Fama and French (1992) and for the momentum effect as identified by Carhart (1997). For example, a fund that focuses on small stocks and value stocks will generate a positive alpha return measured by the capital asset pricing (CAPM) alpha, despite any stock picking talent of the manager. Hence, findings of the CAPM are not robust to the model applied. Markets are efficient enough to prevent alpha returns of institutionally owned REITs in the long run; any such effects are likely explained by risk factors mimicking size and book-to-market effects as well as momentum.

This study's identification strategy emphasizes four key elements for a robust causal inference. First, it accounts for risk factors mimicking size and book-to-market portfolios as well as a momentum factor. The controls we employ explain most of the anomalies identified in the asset pricing literature (Fama, 1998). Second, the identification strategy makes use of Fama and MacBeth (1973) regressions that take into account heteroscedasticity and autocorrelation (Petersen, 2009) and avoid any look-ahead bias. The Fama MacBeth approach works well with panel datasets. It is commonly used for robust inference in asset pricing models. Third, the identification strategy applies changes in institutional ownership instead of levels to avoid for statistical problems related to nonstationarity. Fourth, the fixed-effects regressions remove any unobserved heterogeneity between firms and identify the temporal impact of changes in institutional ownership on market valuations (Tobin's Q) and profitability (return on assets). The estimates make use of a panel of 250 publicly traded US REITs and REOCs. The dataset includes quarterly financial and institutional ownership data for the period 2000 to 2010 and monthly market data for the period 1998 to 2010.

The paper of Bauer et al. (2010) is the newest one to study the relation between corporate governance and REIT performance. It measures the impact of the Corporate Governance Quotient (CGQ) on operating performance measures. Bauer et al. find a weak impact of corporate governance on operating performance. Their reasoning is that REITs operate in a strongly regulated business environment and, therefore, differences in internal corporate governance impact performance only marginally. Our study continues this strand of research by looking at the impact of an external corporate governance mechanism provided by institutional investors. According to the findings of Bauer et al. one would expect the impact of institutional monitoring to be only marginal as well. However, we find that changes of institutional ownership are positively related to both market performance and operating performance. The impact is stronger for firms that exhibit a greater potential for agency issues, which supports the notion that corporate governance is relevant to REITs.

A key finding is that the change in institutional ownership is positively related to three-factor and four-factor alphas in the same quarter. Hence, the stock price rises when there is an increase in institutional ownership, and declines when institutional ownership decreases. The impact of institutional ownership is strongly related to proxies of corporate governance, such as size, profitability and volatility. In particular, REITs/REOCs with a higher sensitivity to agency problems, such as small, unprofitable or volatile firms, benefit more from institutional monitoring and control. A higher level of institutional ownership, however, does not lead to persistent alpha returns.

The remainder of the paper is organized as follows. Section two gives an overview of the studies on institutional ownership in general finance and the real estate literature and presents the associated findings. Section three describes our dataset and discusses the empirical methodology. Section four presents the estimation results. Section five concludes with a summary of the study's most important results.

4.2 Theoretical Background

Institutional ownership of common stock has increased from 32% to 68% between 1980 and 2007 (Lewellen, 2011). Studies on REITs observe rising institutional ownership from 1984 up until 2007, after which institutions' interest in REITs weakened as a result of the subprime crisis (Su Han et al., 1998; Feng et al., 2011).

Institutions that are invested in common stocks and REITs/REOCs include banks, hedge funds, insurance companies, investment advisors, mutual funds and pension funds. They provide monitoring of the management, which leads to improved corporate governance, an associated reduction of agency conflicts (Carleton et al., 1998; Feng et al., 2010) and a higher professionalization of the industry. In particular, institutional participation may (a) lower the cost of capital, (b) ease access to both debt and equity, (c) lower volatility of share prices and (d) facilitate long-term relationships with institutions (Shleifer and Vishny, 1986; Admati et al., 1994; Garrigan and Parsons, 1998; Kahn and Winton, 1998). Institutional investors also act to correct value-destructing actions (see Maug, 1998). An increase in institutional ownership tends to raise demand for a stock, which in turn leads to a higher stock price (Gompers and Metrick, 2001). All of these benefits maximize corporate value, the primary objective of a public company. Therefore, institutional ownership is perceived to be a benefit to a company and its shareholders.

Another strand of the literature perceives that institutional investors "vote with their feet"; they exit when they are dissatisfied with a firm's management

(Admati and Pfleiderer, 2009). Hence, large shareholders are able to reduce agency conflicts through a credible threat of exit. This corporate governance mechanism is weaker for REITs since the IRS rule "five or fewer" prevents large blockholdings.[35]

REITs/REOCs make it easier to identify the impact of institutional ownership on performance as they are a fairly homogenous group of firms with a higher potential for agency issues compared to industrial firms. Agency issues become problematic in the case of pronounced information asymmetries, which should be quite large in the REIT market. This is the result of REITs being typically small firms with lower trading volumes relative to common stock companies (Glascock et al., 1998). Liquidity is lower (Below et al., 1995) and fewer analysts cover REITs (Wang et al., 1995a; Su Han et al., 1998). Damodaran et al. (1993) find that the time gap between the appraisal of properties and its public announcement leads to a temporary information gap between insiders and outsiders. These REIT characteristics are associated with higher information asymmetries, and private information under these circumstances might increase adverse-selection problems. However, uncertainty in the REIT market declined together with transaction costs and liquidity improved in 1994 when the REIT market experienced a large wave of initial public offerings and seasoned equity offerings (Below et al., 1996). REIT cash flow is usually steady and predictable, income statements are fairly transparent, and R&D expenditures are negligible.

---

[35] The "five or fewer" rule (US Internal Revenue Code of 1986, Section 856(a)(6)) prevents five or fewer shareholders from holding 50 percent or more in a REIT.

Benchmark prices from the parallel real estate market are available for comparison and performance evaluation.

The following studies explore the interests of institutional investors for special company characteristics. Institutions prefer to invest in large firms, companies that are part of the S&P 500 and that are low dividend payers (Cready, 1994). Badrinath et al. (1989) find a preference for high beta and an aversion to total risk. The impact of beta is modified by Eakins et al. (1998) to allow for non-linearity. They find that institutions avoid investing in companies at either end of the risk spectrum. Institutions are hesitant to invest in companies whose financial ratios deviate significantly from the mean. Liquidity and low past returns are also preferred characteristics (Gompers and Metrick, 2001). Firms listed on the New York Stock Exchange (NYSE) are preferred and firms listed on the American Stock Exchange (AMEX) are avoided (Eakins et al., 1996). For REITs, Below et al. (2000a) find that institutional ownership depends on beta and firm size. Ciochetti (2002) add liquidity as a driver of institutional ownership. The high importance of these determinants is evidence for the selectivity of institutions to pick firms with particular characteristics. Therefore, it is essential that we control for factors mimicking market, size, book-to-market and momentum effects.

The finance literature provides several studies on the performance of institutional portfolios. Daniel et al. (1997) find that fund managers have a selecting ability but no characteristic timing ability. Cohen et al. (2002) show that institutions buy (sell) in response to positive (negative) cash-flow news; they sell when prices move up in the absence of cash-flow news. This strategy exploits the market's under-reaction to cash flow news. It, however, does not lead to a large deviation relative to the market portfolio and only results in institutions outperforming individuals by 1.44% per annum before transaction costs. Grinblatt and Titman (1989; 1993) find that actively managed funds outperform the market. Newer studies, such as Fama and French (2010), question the superiority of institutional performance altogether. In their view the success of actively managed funds is more a function of luck than the skill of the fund manager. They find that outperforming portfolios balance with underperforming portfolios, which indicates that performance differences result from good luck and bad luck. Institutional investors do not possess better stock-picking skills and their portfolios' net performance (after all costs and fees) closely tracks that of the market portfolio (Lewellen, 2011).

The more sophisticated and robust identification strategies of the newer studies, which adjust for statistical problems of earlier studies and trading costs, reveal the difficulty to generate abnormal returns. They support the efficiency of capital markets. Stock-picking skill is identified with CAPM measures, but the outperformance disappears when controlling for book-to-market and momentum effects (Lewellen, 2011). Likewise, greater institutional ownership in REITs is associated with higher excess returns, benchmark-adjusted returns, Sharpe-ratios and Jensen alphas (Wang et al., 1995b), while it remains unclear whether outperformance is explained by size, book-to-market and momentum effects.

Since the study of Nofsinger and Sias (1999), the finance literature has started to focus on changes in institutional ownership and finds a positive relationship between changes in institutional ownership and risk-adjusted returns. Numerous studies take diverging views on the interpretation of this finding. Three hypotheses are considered to explain this effect: (a) Institutions have information that individual investors do not have and which allows them to time their investment, (b) institutions are short-term momentum traders in that they invest in response to good performance (feedback trading) and (c) institutions move prices due to high-volume trading (Sias et al., 2006).

The current paper fills this research gap for REITs and REOCs by measuring three-factor and four-factor alpha performance of institutional ownership. It also goes a step further by asking whether there is an abnormal return on the event date that is associated with institutional ownership increases. Finally, we examine to what extent the performance impact can be attributed to particular proxies of corporate governance, such as firm size, profitability and volatility.

4.3 Data and Methodology

This study tests (a) whether changes in institutional ownership are positively related to higher values of Tobin's Q and returns on assets, (b) whether changes in institutional ownership lead to higher alphas on the event date and (c) how these effects interact with measures of corporate governance, such as firm size, profitability and volatility. The interactions between the change in institutional ownership and the corporate governance proxies isolate the performance impact of greater institutional monitoring and control. This approach has thus far not been taken in the literature.

The data cover 250 publicly listed US REITs and REOCs for the period 1998Q1 to 2010Q4.[36] We avoid a survivorship bias[37] by including defunct entities that do not exist as separate entities up to the end of the sample because of mergers or acquisitions, or entities that join the sample after 1998Q1 because of a subsequent IPO.

Basic statistics for the model components are found in Table 5. Quarterly financial data and institutional ownership data are derived from the SNL Financial database and monthly stock price data from the Center for Research in Security Prices (CRSP).[38] Monthly data for the return of the S&P 500 index (*MKT*), the 1-month treasury bill return (*RF*), the Fama French factors for the size portfolio (SMB) and book-to-market portfolio (*HML*) and the momentum factor (*UMD*) are obtained from Kenneth French's website at Dartmouth College.[39] The ratios institutional ownership (*IO*) and profitability (return on assets, *ROA*) are winsorized at the 1st and the 99th percentile. In some cases (<1%) institutional ownership is larger than 100% as a result of data issues such as double-counting, short interest and gaps between 'as of' dates.[40] We cope with

---

[36] SNL Financial provides very incomplete data on institutional ownership before 2000.

[37] Survivors tend to be larger and more profitable. They have fewer growth opportunities, higher levels of asset tangibility and higher levels of leverage (Lemmon et al., 2008).

[38] Observations for which there is zero institutional ownership are treated as missing values. This is because we cannot distinguish whether there is no institution invested or if there is no reporting for the respective period in the lists provided by SNL Financial on the institutions invested in REIT. Replacing the missing values with zeros instead would result in zero inflated data that mistakenly identifies missing values as zeros with a strong bias towards the early periods.

[39] http://mba.tuck.dartmouth.edu/pages/faculty/ken.french/

[40] See Appendix 1 for a detailed description of the data issues.

this issue by testing whether setting the maximum ownership of institutions at 100% changes our results as in Lewellen (2011).

Table 5: Variable Definitions and Basic Statistics

Measure	Description	Obs.	Mean	SD	Min	Max
	Quarterly					
IO	Percentage of shares held by institutions	6611	0.534	0.355	0.000	1.274
ΔIO	First difference of IO	6611	0.008	0.073	-0.953	0.922
Size	Market Capitalization	6597	1,814	2,836	-106	29,100
Tobin's Q	(Market capitalization + total liabilities) / (total book equity + total liabilities)	5828	1.317	0.652	0.315	15.753
ROA	Return on assets calculated as net income / total assets	4771	0.007	0.011	-0.044	0.049
	Monthly					
SD	Standard Deviation of R_i-R_f (rolling 24-month windows)	18900	0.094	0.072	0.015	0.674
R_i - R_f	Stock total return minus one-month treasury bill rate	20576	0.011	0.122	-0.866	2.903
RMRF	CRSP US Index (all NYSE, AMEX, and NASDAQ firms) - 30 day US treasury bill rate	20576	-0.001	0.046	-0.170	0.094
SMB	Factor mimicking portfolio for company size	20576	0.002	0.036	-0.222	0.138
HML	Factor mimicking portfolio for book-to-market equity	20576	0.007	0.035	-0.100	0.138
UMD	Factor mimicking portfolio for momentum return	20576	0.088	6.263	-34.750	18.390

Notes: See Appendix 1 for an explanation of *IO* exceeding 100%.

The data indicate a general preference of institutions for REITs/REOCs that are specialized in industrial, specialty, office and residential properties (Table 6). Diversified entities exhibit a much lower institutional ownership. The prominent institutional investors are investment advisors, hedge funds, banks and mutual funds (Table 7).

Table 6: Institutional Ownership Across REIT Property Types

REIT Property Type	No.	Mean Institutional Ownership
Diversified	28	34%
Health Care	17	54%
Hotel	39	50%
Industrial	9	68%
Office	33	60%
Residential	20	64%
Retail	37	53%
Self-Storage	5	58%
Specialty	15	65%
Total	250	53%

Table 7: Institutions' Average Ownership in REITs Across Institution Types

Institution Type	No.	Mean Institutional Ownership
Bank	460	9%
Hedge Fund	688	4%
Insurance	104	2%
Investment Advisor	1788	32%
Mutual Fund	205	22%
Pension Fund	59	4%
Other	39	0%

Notes: The table shows average REIT institutional ownership levels across institution types. *Bank* includes Bank Management Divisions, Brokers and Bank Investment Management. *Other* includes Foundation, Private Banking Portfolios and Arbitrage. The institution type categories are defined by FactSet Research Systems.

The impact of institutional ownership is measured by the three-factor Fama and French (1993) alpha and the four-factor Carhart (1997) alpha. The Fama MacBeth regressions provide a fairly robust model that is applied in several recent studies (e.g. Lewellen, 2011) to measure alpha performance. We apply the Fama MacBeth regressions as follows. Monthly stock data for 250 REITs and REOCs from CRSP and risk factors from the Kenneth French Website for the period 1998 to 2010 are used to calculate factor loadings. To mitigate look-ahead bias, we estimate alpha as a one-month abnormal return, where the factor model loadings are estimated over the prior 24 months of each period.

The monthly rolling regressions (24 month time windows) for the Fama and French model are given as

$$R_{it} - R_{ft} = \propto_{it} + b_{it}RMRF_t + s_{it}SMB_t + h_{it}HML_t + \varepsilon_{it}. \qquad (1)$$

They are run for each observation to estimate the factor loadings b_{it}, s_{it} and h_{it}. R_{it} is the total return of the REIT stock and R_{ft} the US 30-day Treasury Bill rate. $RMRF$ is the return of the S&P 500 minus R_{ft}. SMB_t, HML_t and UMD_t are factor-mimicking portfolios for size, book-to-market equity and one-year momentum in stock returns. The model that augments the Fama French model by the momentum factor suggested by Carhart is formalized as

$$R_{it} - R_{ft} = \propto_{it} + b_{it}RMRF_t + s_{it}SMB_t + h_{it}HML_t + m_{it}UMD_t + \varepsilon_{it}. \qquad (2)$$

We obtain 6,344 factor-loading sets, one for each observation.[41] The equation that calculates alphas via the factor loadings for the Fama French model is given as

$$\propto_{it} = R_{it} - R_{ft} - \hat{b}_{it-1} RMRF_t - \hat{s}_{it-1} SMB_t - \hat{h}_{it-1} HML_t + \varepsilon_{it}. \qquad (3)$$

In analogy, the equation for the alphas from the augmented Fama French model including the Carhart momentum factor is denoted as

$$\propto_{it} = R_{it} - R_{ft} - \hat{b}_{it-1} RMRF_t - \hat{s}_{it-1} SMB_t - \hat{h}_{it-1} HML_t - \widehat{m}_{it-1} UMD_t + \varepsilon_{it}. \qquad (4)$$

To transform monthly data to quarterly data we sum monthly alphas. This reduces the periods to 44 quarters. The following 43 cross-sectional regressions[42] explain alpha as

$$\propto_{it} = a_t + o_t x_{it} + \varepsilon_{it}. \qquad (5)$$

x_{it} is a vector consisting of institutional ownership (*IO*), the first-difference of institutional ownership (*ΔIO*) and interaction terms of *ΔIO* with the natural logarithm of market capitalization (*size*), the return on assets (*ROA*) and the standard deviation of excess stock returns (*SD*). The coefficients of the cross-sectional regressions are then averaged over time, formalized as

$$\bar{o} = \frac{1}{T} \sum_{t=1}^{T} b_t. \qquad (6)$$

[41] To estimate an alpha for each observation we run 12,688 rolling regressions with 24-month estimation windows (6,344 regressions for the Fama French model and 6,344 regressions for the Carhart model).

[42] One period is lost as a result of first-differencing institutional ownership.

P-values are calculated from Fama MacBeth standard errors. These are consistent under heteroscedasticity and serial correlation (Skoulakis, 2006).

To measure the impact of a change in institutional ownership on *Tobin's Q* and return on assets (*ROA*) we apply the firm fixed-effects estimator to account for unobserved heterogeneity across firms. Standard errors are clustered at the firm level to account for heteroscedasticity and serial correlation of errors (Petersen, 2009). Return on assets is a commonly used measure for accounting performance and Tobin's Q for market performance. It is applied in several studies on REIT performance, e.g. in Bauer et al. (2010).

4.4 Estimation Results

There is no empirical evidence that higher overall institutional ownership yields persistent alpha returns (Table 8). Past evidence on statistical significance is likely related to book-to-market, size and momentum effects that are not captured by the CAPM (Fama and French, 2004). In this context, one has to note that persistent alpha returns are unlikely to result from high institutional ownership in an efficient market setting. The reason is that the information about institutional ownership disseminates at the very latest on the mandatory reporting date of each quarter. The information spreads quickly and prices instantly reflect the new information. Therefore, our study focuses on the impact of first differences of institutional ownership on abnormal returns within the robust regression design of Fama and MacBeth (1973).

Table 8: Performance of IO and Δ IO

	FF	Carhart	FF	Carhart	FF	Carhart
IO	0.000	-0.001			0.001	-0.001
	(0.955)	(0.930)			(0.914)	(0.921)
Δ IO			0.077**	0.073*	0.089***	0.080**
			(0.016)	(0.051)	(0.010)	(0.037)
Constant	0.016	0.016	0.018	0.017	0.019	0.019
	(0.204)	(0.266)	(0.308)	(0.339)	(0.131)	(0.155)
Observations	6344	6344	6072	6072	6072	6072

Notes: The table presents coefficients and p-values in parentheses of Fama MacBeth (1973) regressions: Univariate cross-sectional regressions are estimated for each quarter from 2000Q1 to 2010Q4 across all REITs/REOCs. The coefficients are then averaged over time. The dependent variable is the monthly residual from the three-factor (FF) model or the monthly residual from the four-factor (Carhart) model. The factor loadings are estimated for 24-month windows. This way of applying Fama MacBeth Regressions is analogous to Carhart (1997). The independent variables are institutional ownership (*IO*) and change in institutional ownership (*Δ IO*).

Looking at first differences, we find that changes in institutional ownership are positively related to abnormal returns in the three-factor and four-factor models (Table 8). Hence, there are benefits associated with institutional ownership and these benefits are incorporated into the stock price on the quarter the information enters the market. This causes the expectations about the future prospects of a REIT/REOC to change leading to a price appreciation of the company's stock.

The results become even more interesting when one considers interaction terms. The impact of the first difference of institutional ownership on alpha hinges on measures for corporate governance, such as firm size, profitability and volatility (Table 9). Smaller firms, unprofitable firms and firms with high stock price volatility benefit more from institutional ownership. The reason is that such firms are more likely affected by information asymmetries and agency problems, which can be partly alleviated through better monitoring and control by institutional shareholders.

Table 9: Evidence for a Corporate Governance Effect - The Interaction Between Δ IO and Proxies of Corporate Governance

	FF	Carhart	FF	Carhart	FF	Carhart
IO	0.001	-0.001	-0.000	-0.004	0.005	0.002
	(0.895)	(0.943)	(0.990)	(0.663)	(0.627)	(0.812)
Δ IO	0.142***	0.117**	0.083**	0.100**	-0.147	-0.097
	(0.004)	(0.043)	(0.039)	(0.037)	(0.205)	(0.420)
Δ IO * size	-0.005**	-0.005**				
	(0.012)	(0.037)				
size	0.000	-0.000				
	(0.981)	(0.696)				
Δ IO * ROA			-4.337*	-3.979		
			(0.073)	(0.224)		
ROA			-0.347**	-0.294		
			(0.044)	(0.110)		
Δ IO * SD					3.064*	2.760
					(0.077)	(0.112)
SD					0.207**	0.192*
					(0.025)	(0.083)
Constant	0.019	0.020	0.020	0.022	-0.006	-0.005
	(0.105)	(0.120)	(0.151)	(0.147)	(0.399)	(0.612)
Observations	6058	6058	4496	4496	6072	6072

Notes: The table presents coefficients and p-values in parentheses of Fama MacBeth (1973) regressions: Univariate cross-sectional regressions are estimated for each quarter from 2000Q1 to 2010Q4 across all REITs/REOCs. The coefficients are then averaged over time. The dependent variable is the monthly residual from the three-factor (FF) model or the monthly residual from the four-factor (Carhart) model. The factor loadings are estimated for 24-month windows. This way of applying Fama MacBeth Regressions is analogous to Carhart (1997). The interaction term *Δ IO * size* is the product of *Δ IO* and *size*. The interaction term *Δ IO * ROA* is the product of *Δ IO* and *ROA*. The interaction term *Δ IO * SD* is the product of *Δ IO* and *SD*.

The impact of the first difference of institutional ownership on stock market valuation and operating performance is positive. Therefore, an increase in institutional ownership raises Tobin's Q within four quarters and operating profitability within five quarters following an increase in ownership (Table 10 and Figure 4).

Table 10: Impact of Changes in Institutional Ownership on Operating Performance

	ROA	Tobin's Q
ΔIO_{t-1}	0.010***	0.517***
	(0.006)	(0.000)
ΔIO_{t-2}	0.009***	0.460***
	(0.006)	(0.000)
ΔIO_{t-3}	0.014***	0.350***
	(0.000)	(0.001)
ΔIO_{t-4}	0.010***	0.229**
	(0.003)	(0.020)
ΔIO_{t-5}	0.016***	0.090
	(0.000)	(0.311)
ΔIO_{t-6}	0.003	0.063
	(0.486)	(0.415)
ΔIO_{t-7}	0.004	0.100
	(0.251)	(0.176)
ΔIO_{t-8}	-0.000	0.048
	(0.984)	(0.494)
ΔIO_{t-9}	0.008*	-0.010
	(0.088)	(0.872)
ΔIO_{t-10}	0.001	0.091
	(0.793)	(0.121)
Constant	0.006***	1.354***
	(0.000)	(0.000)
Obs	3107	3770
Adjusted R^2	0.32	0.82

Notes: The table presents coefficients and p-values in parentheses of firm fixed-effects regressions with *Tobin's Q* or *ROA* as the dependent variable. The subscripts indicate the lag order, e.g. ΔIO_{t-5} is the fifth lag of ΔIO. Standard errors are robust to heteroscedasticity and autocorrelation. * indicates significance at the 10% level, ** indicates significance at the 5% level, *** indicates significance at the 1% level.

Figure 4: Impact of Changes in Institutional Ownership on Operating Performance

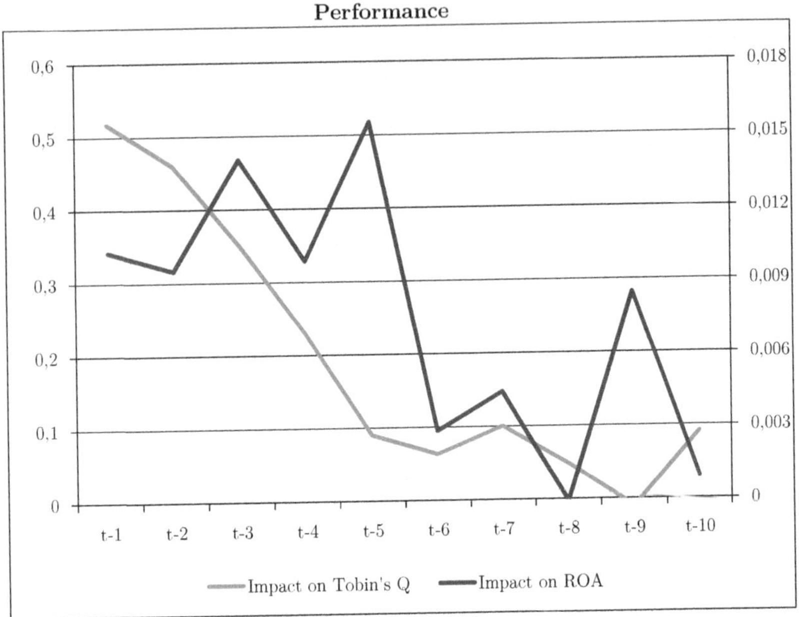

Notes: The graphs plot coefficients of firm fixed-effects regressions from Table 10. The left axis denotes the coefficients for the lags of ΔIO explaining Tobin's Q and the right axis denotes the coefficients for the lags of ΔIO explaining ROA. The time operators on the horizontal axis classify the lag order of ΔIO. Standard errors are robust to heteroscedasticity and autocorrelation.

These results suggest that institutional monitoring can control opportunistic behavior of managers, which may, thereby, lead to a better operating performance. Institutional ownership also reduces the cost of capital, eases access to both debt and equity, lowers volatility of share prices and facilitates long-term relationships with institutions (Gompers and Metrick, 2001). These operating benefits are likely the drivers of the abnormal returns found in the Fama MacBeth regressions on increases in institutional ownership. The positive relationship between changes of institutional ownership and abnormal returns implicitly draws on the assumption that non-institutional demand is constant or does not have a countervailing effect. Changes in demand by institutional investors also impact non-institutional investors because the fraction of shares held by institutional investors is one minus the fraction held by individual investors.

One may argue that the abnormal returns could be related to the price impact of the trade. Price impacts, however, disappear in the short-run. This confounding factor is, therefore, not relevant for our study because we apply data with quarterly frequency. An event study with daily frequency would be affected by the price impact of the trade.

A second argument is that institutional trades cause herding and associated post-herding returns. The following sensitivity analyses test for effects from herding behavior and positive feedback trading that could induce endogeneity in our models. We test for the existence of such an effect and whether this effect changes the conclusions of this study. The models of Table 8 are augmented by a lag of $\Delta\ IO$ in Table 11. The coefficients of $\Delta\ IO_{t-1}$ are insignificant and, therefore, do not provide evidence for a price impact in the period following a change in institutional ownership. This reduces the risk of having herding behavior following institutional trades confounding our results.

A third argument is that positive feedback trading of institutions could explain the positive impact of a change in institutional ownership. Nofsinger and Sias (1999) argue that there is positive feedback trading of institutions for industrial firms. This could explain an abnormal return prior to a change in institutional ownership. To test whether this momentum trading by institutions impact this study's results we run regressions that explain the change in institutional ownership with lagged alphas (Table 12). The insignificant coefficient of lagged abnormal returns provides no indication of momentum trading by institutions.[43]

Table 11: Sensitivity Analysis – Post-Herding Returns

	FF	Carhart
IO	0.000	-0.002
	(0.985)	(0.805)
Δ IO	0.079**	0.079**
	(0.021)	(0.037)
Δ IO_{t-1}	0.050	0.030
	(0.102)	(0.343)
Constant	0.019	0.021
	(0.110)	(0.126)

Notes: The table present coefficients and p-values in parentheses of Fama MacBeth (1973) regressions: Univariate cross-sectional regressions are estimated for each quarter from 2000Q1 to 2010Q4 across all REITs/REOCs (5833 observations). The coefficients are then averaged over time. The dependent variable is the monthly residual from the three-factor (FF) model or the monthly residual from the four-factor (Carhart) model. The factor loadings are estimated for 24-month windows. This way of applying Fama MacBeth Regressions is analogous to Carhart (1997). The independent variables are institutional ownership (*IO*) and change in institutional ownership (*Δ IO*). The subscript for *t-1* indicates the lag order one.

[43] There is a remaining chance that intra-quarter positive feedback trading or post-herding explain the positive abnormal returns that we relate to changes in institutional ownership. Yet, this study's identification strategy accomplishes the best possible isolation of the effect of institutional ownership on alpha returns under the restriction that data on institutional ownership is available only quarterly.

Table 12: Sensitivity Analysis – Positive Feedback Trading

	Model 1	Model 2
FF_Alpha_{t-1}	0.021	
	(0.526)	
$Carhart\_Alpha_{t-1}$		0.019
		(0.440)
Constant	0.006**	0.006**
	(0.026)	(0.027)

Notes: The table presents coefficients and p-values in parentheses of Fama MacBeth (1973) regressions: Univariate cross-sectional regressions are estimated for each quarter from 2000Q1 to 2010Q4 across all REITs/REOCs (6000 observations). The coefficients are then averaged over time. The dependent variable is Δ *IO*. The independent variable is the monthly residual from the three-factor (FF) model or the monthly residual from the four-factor (Carhart) model. The factor loadings are estimated for 24-month windows. This way of applying Fama MacBeth Regressions is analogous to Carhart (1997). The subscript *t-1* indicates the lag of order one.

4.5 Concluding Remarks

Our study evaluates the performance impact of changes in institutional ownership of REITs and REOCs, and to what extent this effect is related to observable characteristics of corporate governance. The study identifies three-factor and four-factor abnormal returns for the period of increasing institutional ownership. Smaller firms, unprofitable firms and volatile firms are affected by greater agency issues and information asymmetries and, therefore, benefit more from additional monitoring and controlling of management by institutional shareholders. The interaction terms between the first difference of institutional ownership and the corporate governance proxies *size*, *profitability* and *volatility* confirm that changes in institutional ownership have a greater impact on alphas for REITs/REOCs that are smaller, unprofitable or volatile.

We also examine past findings of persistent abnormal returns in REITs with high institutional ownership. In accordance with asset pricing theory, REITs/REOCs should not exhibit abnormal returns related to higher institutional ownership in efficient markets. The reason is that the information about institutional ownership and the associated benefits disseminate the latest on the corresponding announcement date of each quarter. Therefore, our study focuses on the impact of changes in institutional ownership on alphas. For this exercise we control for market, size, book-to-market and momentum effects and employ the robust regression design of Fama MacBeth.

Our sensitivity analyses test whether institutional trading cause post-herding returns. A second robustness check tests whether institutions engage in positive feedback trading. The results indicate that neither post-herding following institutional trades nor positive feedback trading by institutions are driving alphas. We conclude that there is no risk for confounding factors in our study.

5 What Drives Institutions to Invest in REITs

5 What Drives Institutions to Invest in REITs

5.1 Introduction

The purpose of this paper is to investigate the macroeconomic and microeconomic factors that drive institutions to invest in real estate investment trusts (REITs). Institutional investors are known for sophisticated investment strategies, monitoring management and identifying investment opportunities. Numerous studies investigate the cross-sectional variation of institutional investment by REIT characteristics to provide a guide on how to tailor an attractive REIT structure. They find firm size among many determinants to be the most prominent driver of institutional REIT investment (Below et al., 2000b; Ciochetti et al., 2002). However, the impact often varies with the time period analyzed (Below et al., 2000b). In particular, the coefficients for financial ratios, such as firm size, market-to-book ratio, return on assets and leverage, are not consistent across time. This suggests that period-specific factors are at work, such as macroeconomic factors or REIT-specific sentiment factors. Institutional investors may also pursue market timing strategies or inflation hedging.

This study addresses the likely time dependence of institutional investments in REITs within the context of a panel data set. In particular, we investigate two questions. First, to what extent do changing macroeconomic conditions affect institutional investors in their decision to buy or sell REITs? Second, are there particular REIT characteristics that drive institutional investment and disinvestment over time?

Knowing the preferences of institutional investors is instrumental to successfully operate REITs. REITs could tailor operating and financial characteristics to a particular institutional clientele to raise their market value. A better understanding of how macroeconomic considerations influence institutional investors could give REITs an understanding of when and why institutional capital is supplied or withdrawn. Knowledge of institutional preferences for certain macroeconomic conditions is beneficial for REITs as it aids them in gauging their accessibility to the equity market. It could also assist institutionally owned REITs in their efforts to time the market more effectively to benefit from stock mispricing.[44]

This study is the first to take macroeconomic factors explicitly into account and to derive causal inferences about the microeconomic determinants of institutional ownership for the REIT market. The identification strategy relies on the firm fixed-effects estimator, which focuses on explaining the within variation of institutional ownership and takes into account any unobserved heterogeneity across firms.[45] The estimates are based on a quarterly panel of 136 publicly traded

[44] See Baker and Wurgler (2002) on the market timing theory that explains the relation of capital structure and market values.

[45] The use of the firm fixed-effects estimator allows the identification of causal inference as opposed to just correlation. It is the primary tool for causal inference in panel data analysis (Angrist and Pischke, 2008).

US REITs for the period 2000 to 2010.

The results of this study suggest that the macroeconomic environment largely determines institutional preference for REITs. In particular, institutional investors prefer REITs when (a) consumer prices are expected to rise because REITs are considered an inflation hedge, (b) interest rates are expected to decrease because particularly the real estate sector gains from attractive financing conditions, and (c) GDP growth is expected to decline because real estate investments are considered a counter-cyclical investment vehicle.

Among the REIT characteristics, leverage is the most important predictor of institutional ownership. Institutional investors invest in REITs when leverage levels are declining and vice versa. They are also attracted by REITs with lower levels of profitability and volatility. Contrary to results from previous cross-section studies size, beta, dividend payout and rating are insignificant. This indicates that REIT efforts to engage in asset growth, reinvest FFO instead of distributing profits, achieve a lower beta or obtain a rating do not necessarily attract institutions over time.

The remainder of the paper is organized as follows. Section two gives an overview of the relevant previous studies on the determinants of institutional ownership and their associated empirical findings. Section three describes the dataset and discusses the empirical methodology. Section four presents the estimation results. Section five concludes with a summary of the study's most important results.

5.2 Theoretical Background

Rising institutional ownership levels in REITs have been reported in the data since 1985 (Su Han et al., 1998). Before 1994, REITs exhibited lower institutional ownership than industrial firms. Su Han et al. (1998) find that starting with the year 1994 the institutional ownership levels recorded for REITs exceed those noted for comparable industrial firms.

This development in the REIT market is viewed as favorable. Institutional ownership benefits REITs mainly for two reasons. First, institutional investors provide monitoring of management and exercise their power through a credible threat of exit[46], which can improve corporate governance and alleviate agency conflicts (Carleton et al., 1998; Feng et al., 2010).[47] This helps to make a company more attractive to investors in general. Yet, this corporate governance mechanism is weaker for REITs because the IRS rule "five or fewer"[48] prohibits

---

[46] Large institutional investors "vote with their feet" to exercise power. A credible threat of exit disciplines managers in their actions. See Admati and Pfleiderer (2009) for an theoretical overview on large shareholder activism.

[47] Agency issues arise in the case of marked information asymmetries. In the REIT market information asymmetries should be quite large. REITs are typically small firms that exhibit lower trading volumes relative to common stock companies (Glascock et al., 1998). Fewer analysts cover REITs (Wang et al., 1995a; Su Han et al., 1998) and liquidity is lower (Below et al., 1995). The appraisal of properties and its public announcement are associated with a temporary information gap in which the management knows the appraisal value while outsiders do not (Damodaran et al., 1993). Such REIT peculiarities result in higher information asymmetries and private information in that respect could create adverse-selection problems. By contrast, REITs also offer transparency advantages: predictable steady cash flows, transparent income statements, negligible R&D expenditures and benchmark prices from the parallel real estate market for comparison and performance evaluation (Below et al., 1996).

[48] The "five or fewer" rule (US Internal Revenue Code of 1986, Section 856(a)(6)) prevents five or fewer shareholders from holding 50 percent or more stock in a REIT.

large blockholdings.

Second, a firm with a larger share of institutional investors may benefit from a lower cost of capital, better access to both debt and equity, and lower volatility of share prices (Garrigan and Parsons, 1998). All of these benefits maximize firm value, which is the primary objective of a public company. Chapter four provided empirical evidence for better performance of REITs that succeed in attracting institutions.

In general, the literature on determinants of institutional investment can be summed up as follows: company size, S&P 500 index affiliation and dividend payout determine institutional ownership (Cready, 1994). In particular, large firms, index constituents and low dividend payers are preferred. Badrinath et al. (1989) identify a preference of institutional investors for high beta and an aversion to total risk. Eakins et al. (1998) allow for a non-linear impact of beta and show that institutions avoid both the least and most risky firms. Their findings also suggest that institutions are reluctant to invest in firms whose leverage and return on assets deviate significantly from the mean. Institutions prefer liquid firms and firms with market underperformance (Gompers and Metrick, 2001). NYSE listed firms are preferred by institutions and firms listed on the AMEX are avoided (Eakins et al., 1996). The institutional investment decisions follow a "herding" pattern in that institutions invest in and disinvest from the same securities (Sias, 2004).

Recent literature on the institutional ownership of REITs (Below et al., 2000b; Below et al., 2000a; Ciochetti et al., 2002) agrees that the positive impact of firm size is the most important driver of institutional ownership. In this vein, Ciochetti et al. (2002) show that institutions are more willing to invest in more liquid REITs, which are typically larger REITs. Below et al. (2000a) and Below et al. (2000b) confirm the impact of company size, but find no consistent impact of beta, market-to-book ratio, leverage, dividend yield and return on assets on institutional ownership across periods via yearly OLS-regressions. The mixed results suggest that period-specific factors are at work.

The methodology applied in previous studies for identifying the determinants of REIT institutional ownership is based on cross-sectional regressions. The regressions explain institutional ownership levels as a function of REIT characteristics. Although this reveals existing correlations and is a useful data reduction technique, it cannot directly address the issue of causality or of changes in the macroeconomic environment, even if the same regression is run for each time period. Our study employs a panel data set along with a fixed-effects estimation methodology that accounts for unobserved heterogeneity among REITs. This allows us to identify how macroeconomic changes impact the decision of institutional investors to invest in REITs. Furthermore, it is possible to address the causal impact of REIT characteristics, such as size, dividend policy, profitability, volatility, beta, performance and leverage, on the level of institutional ownership.

5.3 Data and Methodology

Our data set covers 136 publicly listed US equity REITs (Table 13). The models use quarterly observations from 2000Q1 to 2010Q3. To avoid a survivorship bias[49] we include defunct REITs that do not exist as separate entities up to the end of the sample because of a merger or acquisition or that join the sample after 2000 because of a later IPO.

Table 13: Institutional Ownership Across REIT Property Types

REIT Property Type	No.	Mean Institutional Ownership
Diversified	12	36%
Health Care	12	42%
Hotel	18	37%
Industrial	6	50%
Office	23	50%
Residential	19	50%
Retail	34	40%
Self-Storage	4	41%
Specialty	8	61%
Total	136	44%

Financial data and data on *institutional ownership* are derived from the SNL Financial database. Market data are obtained from the Center for Research in Security Prices (CRSP). The Livingstone Survey[50] of the Federal Reserve Bank of

[49] Survivors tend to be larger and more profitable. They have fewer growth opportunities, higher levels of asset tangibility and higher levels of leverage (Lemmon et al., 2008).

[50] For access to the data of the Livingstone Survey visit the website of the Federal Reserve Bank of Philadelphia (http://www.philadelphiafed.org/research-and-data/real-time-center/livingston-survey/).

Philadelphia provides data on *expected GDP growth*, *expected interest rate change* and *expected inflation*. Historical data on *unemployment* rates are from the Bureau of Labor Statistics. Table 14 lists the variable definitions and the corresponding basic statistics. In a few cases, recorded institutional ownership levels exceed 100%.[51] This can be attributed to data issues, such as gaps between 'as of' dates, short interest and double counting.[52]

Data from the Livingstone Survey are available semi-annually and are reported in June and December each year. Our regression is specified with lagged independent variables to alleviate endogeneity problems. We are faced with two options: one, running semi-annual regressions with a half-year lag of the independents; two, running regressions with quarterly data with a one-quarter lag of the independents.

We choose option two (quarterly frequency) in order to reduce the lag, because institutional investors adjust their investments quickly to changes in their expectations. A six-month lag would imply that institutional investors react with a long delay, an unrealistic assumption. They are, in fact, guided by fundamental corporate figures from the latest quarterly reports and their most recent macroeconomic expectations. Hence, the lag of the explanatory variables should be as short as possible.

---

[51] Less than 1% of the data on institutional ownership is affected. We adjust the scale of *institutional ownership* by dividing all its values by its maximum of 133%. To check for robustness of this approach we run regressions with *institutional ownership* capped at 100%. The different approaches do not yield materially different results.

[52] See Appendix 1 for a detailed description of the data issues.

Table 14: Variable Definitions and Basic Statistics

Variable	Description	Mean	SD	Min	Max
Institutional Ownership	Percentage of shares held by institutions	0.438	0.268	0.000	1.000
Expected GDP Growth	Expected change in US real gross domestic product	0.030	0.007	0.004	0.042
Expected Interest Rate Change	Expected change in the US prime interest rate	0.117	0.114	-0.053	0.316
Unemployment	US unemployment rate	0.057	0.017	0.038	0.099
Expected Inflation	Expected change in the US consumer price index (CPI)	0.022	0.003	0.017	0.027
Excess Market Return	S&P 500 total return minus risk free rate	0.012	0.094	-0.238	0.147
Trend	Counts from 1 to 43 from 2000Q1 to 2010Q3	22	12	1	43
Market-to-Book	Market value of equity / book value of equity	1.585	1.125	0.000	8.089
Size	Natural logarithm of total assets deflated by the US CPI	7.424	0.776	5.410	9.786
Asset Tangibility	Real estate assets / total assets	0.828	0.108	0.275	0.983
Return on Assets	Net income / total assets	0.009	0.009	-0.044	0.049
Earnings Volatility	Percentage change in net income	0.005	0.154	-1.970	3.461
Stock Volatility	Standard deviation of excess returns.	0.078	0.055	0.016	0.603
Beta	CAPM-beta	0.756	0.749	-1.715	4.734
Dividend Payout	Dividends / funds from operations	0.709	0.288	0.000	1.962
Δ Stock Price	Change in raw stock price	0.020	0.178	-0.915	1.813
Rating	1 if REIT is rated by S&P, Moody's or Fitch, and 0 otherwise	0.448	0.497	0.000	1.000
S&P 500 Constituency	1 if REIT is in S&P 500, and 0 otherwise	0.065	0.247	0.000	1.000
Leverage	Financial debt / (market value of equity + financial debt)	0.472	0.170	0.001	0.932

Notes: 1929 observations are available for each variable. The ratios *institutional ownership, leverage, market-to-book, asset tangibility* and *profitability* are winsorized at the 1st and the 99th percentile.

Along these lines, we choose quarterly frequency for the regressions which reduces the lag to three months and assigns the Livingstone Survey data for June to quarter two (Q2) and that for December to quarter four (Q4). Because we do not have data from the Livingstone Survey for March or September we have to drop out quarter one (Q1) and quarter three (Q3) for the other explanatory variables. We end up with data on *institutional ownership* for Q1 and Q3 on the left-hand side of the regression. The values on the left-hand side for Q1 are matched with the explanatory variables for Q4 of the previous year, which gives a one-quarter lag. The left-hand side values for Q3 are matched with Q2 right-hand side values of the same year. To test for robustness of the regression results, in particular the existence of a bias due to quarter-specific effects, we also run quarterly models on all observations and replace the macroeconomic variables with quarterly time fixed-effects.

For a first look at the data we identify the average institutional ownership levels across the quintiles of REIT characteristics. This gives an indication on how institutional ownership correlates with its various determinants. In particular, the quantile results of Table 15 show that higher values of *market-to-book*, *size* and *beta* go in tandem with higher levels of *institutional ownership*. *Dividend payout* and *asset tangibility* are negatively related to levels of *institutional ownership*. Institutions further appear to favor REITs that are rated or that are constituents of the S&P 500 index (Table 16). The indications for *stock volatility*, *leverage* and *beta* for REITs show that institutions are considerate of the appearance of their portfolio and, therefore, avoid extremes.

Table 15: Institutional Ownership by Quintiles of REIT Characteristics

Quintiles	Low	2	3	4	High	High - Low
Market-to-Book	36%	43%	44%	51%	46%	10%***
Beta	35%	44%	47%	49%	44%	9%***
Stock Volatility	39%	46%	49%	47%	39%	0%
Δ Stock Price	39%	46%	46%	47%	41%	2%
Asset Tangibility	47%	47%	47%	41%	37%	-10%***
Size	22%	40%	51%	51%	55%	33%***
Leverage	41%	52%	43%	45%	38%	-3%
Dividend Payout	49%	51%	45%	39%	35%	-14%***
Return on Assets	39%	47%	49%	44%	39%	0%

Notes: The table presents average *institutional ownership* by quintiles of *market-to-book*, *beta*, *stock volatility*, *Δ stock price*, *asset tangibility*, *size*, *leverage*, *dividend payout* and *return on assets*. E.g. in the third quintile of *market-to-book* the average *institutional ownership* is 44%. The quintiles are calculated separately for each quarter. *High – Low* shows the difference between the means of *institutional ownership* of the highest quantile and the lowest quantile of the respective firm characteristic. E.g. the means of *institutional ownership* of the high and low *market-to-book* quantiles differ by 10% with significance at the 1% level. * indicates significance at the 10% level, ** indicates significance at the 5% level, *** indicates significance at the 1% level.

Table 16: Institutional Ownership by Rating and S&P 500 Constituency

	No	Yes	Yes - No
Rating	41%	62%	21%***
S&P 500 Constituency	35%	52%	17%***

Notes: The table presents average *institutional ownership* by *rating* (0/1) and *S&P 500 constituency* (0/1). E.g. REITs with a *rating* have on average an *institutional ownership* of 62%. *Yes – No* shows the difference in the means of *institutional ownership* between rated and non-rated REITs in the second row and between S&P 500 constituents and non-constituents in the third row. E.g. the means of *institutional ownership* between the rated and non-rated REITs differ by 21% with significance at the 1% level. * indicates significance at the 10% level, ** indicates significance at the 5% level, *** indicates significance at the 1% level.

We make use of a firm fixed-effects estimator to test for a causal impact of each determinant.[53] This approach controls for any unobserved heterogeneity across firms and alleviates a potential omitted variable bias involved in cross-sectional studies. Standard errors are clustered at the firm level to account for heteroscedasticity and serial correlation of errors (Petersen, 2009).

A broad set of proxies for firm characteristics is applied: the determinants *market-to-book, leverage, size* and *dividend payout* are analogous to Below et al. (2000b) and Ciochetti et al. (2002) and *beta* is analogous to Below et al. (2000a). We further add *asset tangibility, return on assets, rating, S&P 500 constituency, Δ stock price, stock volatility* and *earnings volatility* to the equation.

Market-to-book measures growth opportunities of firms (Frank and Goyal, 2009) and is intended to provide information on whether institutions have a preference for growth. It also measures the market valuation of a firm and, therefore, can be considered a proxy for market timing behavior of institutions.

Historical operating and market performance are usually criteria for all investors. The variables *return on assets* and *Δ stock price* account for these effects.

REITs that are part of the S&P 500 index (*S&P 500 constituency*) or carry a *rating* may be attractive for a clientele interested in high transparency and

[53] The pooled model is tested against the random effects model via the Breusch-Pagan test. The test confirms, at better than the one percent level, that the simple pooled regression is rejected relative to the random effects model. The random effects model, in turn, is tested against the firm fixed-effects model via the Hausman test. The random effects model is rejected in favor of the firm fixed-effects model.

analyst coverage. Additionally, we measure the coefficient for *dividend payout* to account for a preference for dividends or capital gains.

Leverage is incorporated in the models to consider institutional preference for a certain capital structure. Some institutions bear leverage restrictions that could limit the pool of REITs eligible for an investment.

Firm *size* is the most frequently mentioned determinant of institutional ownership in the literature. It is expected that institutional investors select larger REITs as they typically offer more liquidity and lower trading costs. To proxy for portfolio liquidity we employ *asset tangibility*, which is the fraction of real estate assets to total assets.

Beta gives insight into the attitude of institutional investors towards systematic risk, whereas *stock volatility* measures the general disposition to return volatility. For operating volatility we employ the proxy *earnings volatility*.

One key contribution of this study is to identify the effects macroeconomic factors have on the level of institutional investments in REITs. The model includes proxies for *expected inflation*, *expected interest rate change*, *expected GDP growth*, *unemployment* and *excess market return* of the S&P 500 index.

Institutions may have an interest in diversifying their portfolio with REITs to hedge the risk of inflation. REITs are an inflation-hedging tool that may offer substantially higher returns than Treasury Inflation-Protected Securities (TIPS). REITs often have step-up clauses in their leases, which allow rent increases to counter inflation. They, however, are not an equally effective inflation hedge as TIPS. The more effective inflation protection of TIPS is at the costs of lower returns. The choice of the inflation hedge eventually depends on the preference of the investor.

REIT can also serve investors as a low beta investment when the economy (GDP growth) and the general stock market (S&P 500) are expected to decline and unemployment rises. Despite a relatively high correlation of REITs with the general stock market in the short term (e.g. monthly), they are less correlated on longer investment horizons (a quarter or more). We expect institutional investors, which typically target REITs as a long-term investment, to appreciate the diversification ability of REITs.

We suggest institutions consider debt market conditions as well. REITs typically perform well in low-interest environments because their highly leveraged capital structures result in a strong dependence on the debt market. In low-interest environments REITs obtain attractive financing for long-term debt via fixed interest rates.

The introduced macro factors take an appropriate specification for an investment managers' point of view that forecasts firm profits in conjunction with economic expectations. The choice of expected values allows for an interesting forward-looking perspective. Using actual economic figures in lieu of expected figures in our models would explain less of the variation of institutional ownership.[54]

---

[54] The adjusted R-squared of the model with expected macroeconomic figures is 0.914 and the model with actual macroeconomic figures is 0.910. Hence, the expected figures provide a better fit

Figure 5: Time-Series Institutional Ownership of US Equity REITs

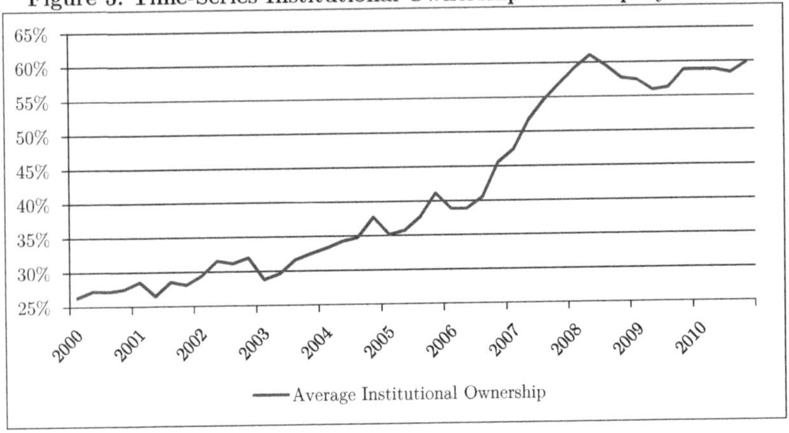

Institutional investors have continuously increased their stake in REITs for the study period (Figure 5). A *trend* variable controls for the positive trend that impacts all REITs. It counts from 1 to 43 for the quarterly periods 2000Q1 to 2010Q3.

5.4 Estimation Results

The decision of institutional investors to hold REITs in their portfolios depends on both macroeconomic and microeconomic factors (see Table 17). The variance decomposition shows that most of the variation in the dependent variable can be attributed to just one determinant, *leverage*. *Leverage* also turns out to have the highest elasticity among the covariates. The detailed findings are discussed in the following.

---

for modeling the impact of macroeconomic conditions on institutional ownership.

Table 17: Fixed-Effects Regressions Explaining Institutional Ownership

	Property Type Fixed-Effects Model	Firm Fixed-Effects Model	Restricted Firm Fixed-Effects Model
Expected GDP Growth	-3.132***	-1.609***	-1.721***
	(0.000)	(0.000)	(0.000)
Expected Interest Rate Change	-0.016	-0.050***	-0.057***
	(0.583)	(0.006)	(0.001)
Unemployment	0.459	0.830*	0.909**
	(0.571)	(0.083)	(0.018)
Expected Inflation	9.356***	4.474***	4.787***
	(0.000)	(0.000)	(0.000)
Excess Market Return	0.025	0.017	
	(0.405)	(0.189)	
Trend	0.014***	0.007***	0.008***
	(0.000)	(0.002)	(0.000)
Leverage	-0.161**	-0.281***	-0.273***
	(0.044)	(0.000)	(0.000)
Market-to-Book	-0.005	-0.004	
	(0.668)	(0.357)	
Size	0.142***	-0.018	
	(0.000)	(0.682)	
Asset Tangibility	-0.078	-0.086	
	(0.618)	(0.367)	
Return on Assets	-1.872**	-0.603*	-0.537*
	(0.045)	(0.073)	(0.073)
Earnings Volatility	0.008	-0.011	
	(0.775)	(0.308)	
Stock Volatility	-0.175	-0.244**	-0.228**
	(0.510)	(0.047)	(0.016)
Beta	0.030	-0.000	
	(0.115)	(0.973)	
Dividend Payout	-0.139***	-0.008	
	(0.000)	(0.528)	
Δ Stock Price	-0.018	-0.029**	-0.025**
	(0.495)	(0.026)	(0.027)
Rating	0.061	-0.013	
	(0.134)	(0.570)	
S&P 500 Constituency	-0.085**	-0.049**	-0.047**
	(0.043)	(0.025)	(0.031)
Constant	-1.261***	0.338	0.075
	(0.002)	(0.455)	(0.165)
Adjusted R^2	0.441	0.914	0.913

Notes: The table presents coefficients and p-values in parentheses of fixed-effects regressions including 1929 observations with *institutional ownership* as the dependent variable. Standard errors are robust to heteroscedasticity and autocorrelation. * indicates significance at the 10% level, ** indicates significance at the 5% level, *** indicates significance at the 1% level.

Among the macroeconomic factors, *expected GDP growth*, *unemployment*, *expected interest rate change* and *expected inflation* drive institutions to invest in REITs (see Table 17). In particular, institutional ownership is positively related to *expected inflation* and *unemployment* and negatively related to *expected GDP growth* and *expected interest rate change*.

This suggests that institutional investors choose REITs intentionally as an inflation hedge.[55] The impact of *expected interest rate change* shows that institutional investors choose REITs when interest rates are expected to go down. The economic rationale is that REITs benefit more from favorable financing conditions than industrial firms do. REITs are typically highly leveraged and, therefore, the profitability of investments depends especially on the conditions of the debt market. They enter into long-term debt arrangements with fixed interest rates, which enable them to fix favorable interest rates for the term of the real estate investment. REITs serve institutions as a counter-cyclical investment vehicle when GDP growth is expected to decline. This counter-cyclical market timing behavior is supported by the positive impact of the variable *unemployment* on *institutional ownership*. The low long-term correlation of REITs with the general stock market appears to be appreciated by institutions.

Among the microeconomic factors, low values of *leverage*, *return on assets*, *stock volatility* and *Δ stock price* motivate institutions to invest in REITs and vice versa (see Table 17). Institutions avoid REITs with high *leverage* because

[55] That REITs can be an inflation hedge is found by Glascock et al. (2002).

many institutional investors face leverage restrictions. Institutions choose REITs with lower past operating performance (*return on assets*) and lower past market performance (*Δ Stock Price*). This predicted behavior of institutions is different from that observed in previous findings for industrial firms: Grinblatt et al. (1995) shows that the majority of institutions are momentum investors. The finding of this study that REIT underperformers are preferred indicates that institutions seek REITs that exhibit a potential for agency conflicts for which they can provide monitoring of the management.[56] Institutions provide such monitoring to foster the performance of their investment.

This shareholder activism is found to have a significant effect on corporate value (Edmans and Manso, 2011). Individual investors are limited in engaging in monitoring management, typically due to their smaller stake and limited expertise. They do, however, benefit from the monitoring of institutions without bearing any of the related costs.[57] The negative relationship of *institutional ownership* to operating and market performance also means that there is no evidence of any positive feedback trading of institutional investors[58] or of any associated negative feedback trading of individuals for REITs, or that these effects at least offset each other.

The aversion of institutional investors to *stock volatility* indicates that they

[56] In a similar vein, Smith (1996) shows that shareholder activism is larger for poor performing industrial firms.

[57] The implications of such a free-rider phenomenon are studied in Ang et al. (2000).

[58] Nofsinger and Sias (1999) find positive feedback trading of institutional investors for industrial firms.

select less risky REITs. Institutions typically measure risk with the value at risk (VaR) approach, which is based on historical volatility, to calculate their capital structure. In this sense, a REIT investment with lower historical volatility qualifies for higher leverage. Individual investors, however, favor riskier stocks with high trading volume and extreme one-day returns (Barber and Odean, 2008).

For an appropriate interpretation of the findings one has to note that institutional ownership is the flip side of individual ownership. The fraction of shares held by institutional investors is one minus the fraction held by individual investors. Therefore, an increase in institutional ownership does not necessarily mean that institutional demand increases. It could also be brought about by an increasing demand of individual investors. For example, the negative relationship between *S&P 500 constituency* and *institutional ownership* is likely caused by a greater popularity of index-REITs among individual investors. Individual investors tend to invest in REITs that have greater media coverage and popularity, such as index-REITs. This result is consistent with the view of Barber and Odean (2008) that individual investors are typically unsophisticated, trade on "glitter"-stocks and on stocks in the news. Therefore, the aforementioned impact of *S&P 500 constituency* is less likely to result from a reluctance of institutional investors to REITs that belong to the S&P 500 index. Yet, institutional investors appear less impressed by a REIT's entry into an index. Continuing the thought, institutions prefer to buy a REIT before it becomes part of an index, which indicates a better knowledge of institutional investors.

The impacts of *size*, *beta*, *dividend payout* and *rating* on institutional investment in REITs, as reported in the literature, are insignificant when we control for firm fixed-effects. Our findings confirm the positive impact of *size* and the negative impact of *dividend payout* from past studies only in the property type fixed-effect model that accounts for unobserved heterogeneity across property types but neglects unobserved heterogeneity across firms. This suggests that REITs that attempt to attract investors by pushing asset growth (*size*), lowering *dividend payout*, obtaining a *rating* or adjusting *beta* should not expect a greater popularity among institutional investors. The study of Bennett et al. (2003) identifies the impact of *size* to be negative over time for industrial firms, a finding counter the common notion that institutional investors consider a large firm size a prime selection criterion. In the REIT literature the positive relation of *size* has not yet been called into question. Our study finds the impact of *size* not existent in the fixed-effects model. Neither the negative feedback of Bennett et al. (2003) nor the positive feedback found by Cready (1994) to changes in *size* is confirmed for REITs.

The economic interpretation of the impact of the determinants is illustrated through elasticity tables and their variance contribution through a variance decomposition. The elasticity at the mean offers a convenient economic interpretation of the impact of the covariates: the expected percent change of institutional ownership as a result of a one percent change in an explanatory variable. This allows a standardized comparison of the effects.

We employ analyses of covariance to measure the fraction of the explained variance in institutional ownership that is attributable to each one of its determinants.[59] In practice, the partial sum of squares of each determinant is divided by the total sum of squares of all determinants other than the fixed-effects and the *trend* variable.[60]

The variance decomposition shows that *leverage* is the most important driver of institutional ownership in the firm fixed-effects model (Table 18).[61] Hence, changes in *leverage* are instrumental in understanding why institutions enter or exit a REIT investment. *Expected GDP growth* and *S&P 500 constituency* rank second and third.

The elasticity estimates show that a 10% increase in *leverage* results in a 3% decrease in institutional ownership (Table 19).[62] This is the largest impact among the determinants. The financial crisis likely contributed to the strong variation of REIT *leverage*. Yet, the finding is robust to the period analyzed. Restricting the regressions to the period that excludes the volatile quarters during the financial crisis does not materially change the results. *Expected inflation* has the second highest elasticity; a 10% change in *expected inflation* causes a 2.3% increase of *institutional ownership*.

---

[59] This decomposes the variation of the dependent variable as in Lemmon et al. (2008).

[60] Type III sum of squares are appropriate, because Type I sum of squares are susceptible to the covariates' ordering as it sequentially projects the dependent variable onto each independent variable, and we use unbalanced data.

[61] A graphical illustration on how the variance contributions of each factor compare can be found in Appendix 3 for the macroeconomic factors and in Appendix 4 for the REIT characteristics.

[62] A graphical illustration on how the elasticity estimates of each factor compare can be found in Appendix 5 for the macroeconomic factors and in Appendix 6 for the REIT characteristics.

Table 18: Variance Decomposition: Analysis of Covariance

	Property Type Fixed-Effects	Firm Fixed-Effects
Expected GDP Growth	0.042	0.101
Expected Interest Rate Change	0.000	0.021
Unemployment	0.001	0.030
Expected Inflation	0.018	0.042
Excess Market Return	0.000	0.002
Leverage	0.055	0.563
Market-to-Book	0.003	0.009
Size	0.537	0.012
Asset Tangibility	0.008	0.026
Return on Assets	0.025	0.022
Earnings Volatility	0.000	0.003
Stock Volatility	0.003	0.050
Beta	0.017	0.000
Dividend Payout	0.167	0.003
Δ Stock Price	0.001	0.023
Rating	0.077	0.011
S&P 500 Constituency	0.046	0.080
Adjusted R^2	0.38	0.90

Notes: The table presents the quotients of each effect's partial sum of squares divided by the total sum of squares of all factors (except the fixed-effects and the control variable *trend*). This forces the columns to sum to one. It identifies the fraction of sum of squares that are attributable to one particular effect. A *trend* variable is included in all models to control for the positive time trend of *institutional ownership* that impact all REITs.

Table 19: Elasticity Estimates

	Property Type Fixed-Effects	Firm Fixed-Effects
Expected Real GDP Growth	*-0.212*	*-0.109*
Expected Interest Rate Change	*-0.004*	*-0.013*
Unemployment	0.060	*0.108*
Expected Inflation	*0.472*	*0.226*
Excess Market Return	0.001	0.000
Leverage	*-0.174*	*-0.303*
Market-to-Book	-0.018	-0.015
Size	*0.142*	-0.018
Asset Tangibility	-0.148	-0.163
Return on Assets	*-0.038*	*-0.012*
Earnings Volatility	0.000	0.000
Stock Volatility	-0.031	*-0.044*
Beta	0.052	-0.001
Dividend Payout	*-0.225*	-0.012
Δ Stock Price	-0.001	*-0.001*

Notes: The table presents the elasticities of the covariates. E.g. a positive 10% change in leverage in the firm fixed-effects model results in a positive 3% change in institutional ownership. A *trend* variable is included in all models to control for the positive time trend of institutional ownership that impact all REITs. Italics indicate significance at the 10% level.

The last column of Table 17 contains a restricted version of the full model in the previous column. All statistically insignificant variables are removed in the restricted model version.[63] This improves the statistical efficiency of the estimates and focuses the economic interpretation. The restricted model with firm fixed-effects is given as

[63] An F-test for the joint statistical significance of all zero restrictions generates a p-value of 0.656. This indicates that the joint zero restrictions are not rejected by the data.

$$\begin{aligned} \textit{Institutional Ownership}_{it} = {} & b_0 + b_1 \textit{Expected GDP Growth}_{it} \\ & + b_2 \textit{Expected Interest Rate Change}_t + b_3 \textit{Unemployment}_{it} \\ & + b_4 \textit{Expected Inflation}_{it} + b_5 \textit{Trend}_{it} + b_6 \textit{Leverage}_{it} \\ & + b_7 \textit{Return on Assets}_{it} + b_8 \textit{Stock Volatility}_{it} + b_9 \Delta\, \textit{Stock Price}_{it} \\ & + b_{10} \textit{S\&P } 500\ \textit{Constituency}_{it} + c_i + \varepsilon_{it}. \end{aligned} \tag{7}$$

This study uses mean differencing to implement the fixed-effects estimator. Mean differencing in lieu of dummy variable regressions is appropriate to save degrees of freedom. For purely illustrative reasons we use firm dummies (c_i) in equation 7. It is interesting to note in this context that the firm fixed-effects capture a large portion of the variation of REIT institutional ownership.[64] This indicates that institutional ownership levels are primarily driven by an unobserved time-invariant REIT fixed-effect. Institutional ownership levels are stable and specific to each individual REIT. Property type fixed-effects, in contrast, explain only a small fraction of institutional ownership, about five percent.[65] This means that there are few time-invariant REIT fixed-effects related to the property type of the portfolio.

The coefficients for the determinants *size, beta, dividend payout* and *rating* are insignificant and, therefore, the variables are excluded in equation 7. Their effects appear significant only in a cross-sectional setting, but not when controlling for

[64] A model that regresses institutional ownership only on firm fixed-effects explains 77% of the variation.

[65] A model that regresses institutional ownership only on property type fixed-effects explains 5% percent of the variation.

firm fixed-effects; causal inference in this case is not appropriate.

As a robustness check we run regressions that include all quarters without the data from the Livingstone survey. These additional regressions test whether the selection of quarters two and four for the independent variable and quarters one and three for the dependent variable results in a bias. Our results do not materially change for these specifications.

To check whether our macro variables are appropriate proxies for any macroeconomic effects that impact all REITs, we use time fixed-effects in lieu of macroeconomic variables. The outcome is that the different models have effectively the same adjusted R-squared. The difference in R-squared is only 0.005, which is negligible. We conclude that our macroeconomic variables capture the close to all variation across time that is relevant for the explanation of institutional investors and their desire to invest in REITs.

5.5 Concluding Remarks

This paper contributes to the literature on the determinants of REIT institutional ownership. It is motivated by (a) the lack of studies that consider macroeconomic effects in explaining institutional investment and (b) our interest in identifying causal linkages between institutional ownership and typical REIT characteristics, such as firm size or leverage. To be able to capture macro effects and establish causality we employ a panel data set and use a fixed-effects estimator as our identification strategy. Variance decompositions and elasticity estimates provide more detail on the statistical and economic magnitude of the effects.

The results provide strong evidence that macroeconomic factors are important drivers behind institutional investment in REITs. Adding the expectations about the developments of GDP, inflation and interest rates to the determinants of institutional investments in REITs appears to be a significant contribution to the literature. The results are not only statistically significant but also offer new economic insights. In particular, an expected weaker economy in terms of GDP growth and unemployment appears to be a motivation for institutions to invest in REITs as opposed to in industrial firms. REIT investments must be perceived as reducing the exposure of institutional investors to the general stock market. Institutions also appear to perceive REITs as an inflation hedge and, therefore, invest when inflation expectations are high. Institutional investors also see REITs as winners of favorable financing conditions. This makes REITs attractive in times of low interest rates.

These results provide a guide for future research on how institutional investment decisions hinge on market conditions. We show that our four macroeconomic variables turn out to explain most of what standard time fixed-effects would capture. This shows that we are not losing important information by using explicit macroeconomic variables. On the contrary, our model with macroeconomic variables provides new information on the behavior of institutional investors.[66]

[66] Applying time fixed-effects involves a loss of informational content in that firm-invariant variables, such as proxies for the macroeconomy, are excluded from the panel regressions and their impacts can no longer be measured. The incorporation of macroeconomic variables in lieu of time

The current expectations about the macroeconomy in the US are characterized by fears about inflation, continued unemployment and low GDP growth while interest rates are at a record low. According to our findings, institutions prefer a REIT investment in such an environment. Hence, REIT institutional ownership is likely to increase in the near future as a result of macroeconomic factors.

The findings on the microeconomic factors show a negative impact on institutional ownership for the determinants *leverage, return on assets, stock volatility, Δ stock price* and *S&P 500 constituency* in the firm fixed-effects model. The cross-sectional dependence of *size* and *beta* found in the REIT literature (Below et al., 2000b; Below et al., 2000a; Ciochetti et al., 2002) and of *dividend payout* found in the general finance literature (Cready, 1994) are not confirmed in the firm fixed-effects model for REITs. We, therefore, conclude that causal inference is not appropriate. Another new and interesting finding is the strong impact of *leverage* on the willingness of institutional investors to buy into REITs. The negative impact of *leverage* drives most of the explained variation of *institutional ownership*. This indicates that leverage restrictions of institutions have become critical for investment decisions; earlier studies on REITs did not find a significant effect of *leverage* on *institutional ownership*.

fixed-effects is only acceptable if the macroeconomic variables resemble the explanatory power of the time fixed-effects. For our study the difference in the explanatory power of both specifications are marginal (difference in terms of R-squared is 0.005) and, therefore, give evidence for a good fit of our macro variable choice.

6 Summary, Practical Implications, and Outlook

The research papers of this dissertation contribute to the existing body of REIT literature on corporate governance in three major ways: Paper one focuses on an agency conflict in the REIT market for the period prior to 1993 and shows how managerial opportunistic behavior has been mitigated as a result of enhanced monitoring and increasing awareness of governance issues. The second paper identifies the impact of institutional ownership on REITs attaining higher corporate profitability and value. Paper three studies how REITs can attract institutions to benefit from the associated monitoring and corporate control. The following gives an overview of the most important findings of our research, highlights the contributions to the literature, emphasizes the practical relevance and points to further research.

Paper one finds that externally advised REITs choose lower leverage levels than their internally advised counterparts for the new REIT era (since 1993), a finding that contrasts with the results of Capozza and Seguin (2000) on the presence of agency problems in externally advised REITs for the era prior to 1993. Our findings make economic sense considering the fact that externally advised REITs bear a higher cost of debt. Therefore, there is no reason to suspect an agency problem for externally advised REITs related to the capital structure in the REIT era since 1993. The fact that some REITs decide to continue to operate with the external advisor structure is evidence that trust has been regained and some investors appreciate the benefits that externally advised REITs can have, such as scale effects, due to advisors managing multiple REITs, and access to a large pool of qualified employees. It appears that the more sophisticated environment of the new REIT era monitors the behavior of external advisors more effectively and, therefore, drives external advisors to make competitive and prudent investment decisions with less opportunistic motivation.

Corporate governance in REITs has also improved as a result of greater institutional investment. This finding of *paper two* is especially interesting considering that the REIT market is highly regulated and corporate governance should be rather homogenous across all REITs. Yet, we identify a significantly positive relationship between risk-adjusted returns (alphas) and changes in institutional ownership. This impact hinges on measures for corporate governance such as firm size, profitability and volatility, that is, on interactions not identified in previous studies; smaller firms, unprofitable firms and firms with high stock price volatility gain more from institutional ownership in the context of corporate governance. In accordance, an increase in institutional ownership yields larger values for Tobin's Q and return on assets in the five quarters following an increase in institutional ownership. To paraphrase these results, capital markets appreciate the participation of institutional investors in securitized real estate because they anticipate an improvement in operating performance. The expected greater operating profitability due to institutional ownership is likely a result of an improved access to financing, reduced cost of capital and lower stock price volatility. These factors are especially important considering that REITs are strongly dependent on capital markets, because their ability to finance themselves from internal funds is limited as a result of the dividend payout requirement. The limited market for corporate control of REITs is a further indicator of the need for institutional activism. This suggests that REITs should intensify their relationships with institutions and develop business models in this direction. In particular, real estate trusts that are still small and suffer from higher volatility and poor operating performance should engage in attracting institutional investors to commit themselves to greater monitoring and governance.

The current literature on the drivers of institutional investment in REITs primarily focuses on firm size. However, it has not been clear whether increasing institutional ownership is a result of firm size, or firm size increases following greater interest from institutions. Cross-sectional studies in the REIT literature did not manage to isolate this effect. *Paper three* is the first study to identify causal relationships for the determinants of institutional ownership to give REITs a guide on how to attract institutional investment for the development of a successful growth strategy and to commit themselves to greater monitoring. The paper also extends the current literature by taking into account macroeconomic conditions as institutional investors are found to be timing the market (Busse and Bollen, 2001).

We complement studies on the motivational drivers of institutional investment by showing that the results of cross-sectional studies on the impacts of firm size, beta and dividend payout on institutional ownership are not confirmed in a robust panel setting and, hence, do not allow for reliable causal inference. This finding is unique and contrary to the evidence in the literature. We suggest future research in this field to account for unobserved heterogeneity across REITs through a firm fixed-effects approach. The importance of macroeconomic determinants identified in our study, substantiates the need to control for at least time fixed-effects. For disentangling the time fixed-effects into its components, we suggest incorporating expected values for economic growth, interest rates and inflation into the models. Neglecting such effects are likely to result in endogeneity problems.

The results of paper three further contribute to the existing body of the literature by finding that institutional ownership is positively related to expected inflation and unemployment, and negatively related to expected interest rate changes and expected GDP growth. This suggests that institutions favor REITs particularly in weaker economic times. The low correlation of the underlying real estate assets with the general stock market makes REITs an attractive investment for the purpose of diversification. Our empirical evidence further indicates that institutions tend to hold REIT-stocks to hedge against inflation, despite the fact that Treasury Inflation-Protected Securities (TIPS) provide the most effective inflation hedge but at the cost of lower returns. Institutions consider debt market conditions too; they increasingly invest when REITs benefit from low interest rates. The knowledge of these macroeconomic drivers can provide REIT managers with a better idea of the availability of financing from institutions and additional skills for market timing.

Among the microeconomic effects, profitability and past stock performance are negatively related to institutional ownership. Our findings suggest a preference of institutions for REITs that underperform, which, in turn, provides these REITs with stronger monitoring and corporate control. Institutions usually support turnaround measures, urge corrective actions and eliminate unnecessary risks. Institutions do not pursue altruistic goals in these efforts but follow a strategy that maximizes the return on their investment; they expect the value of their investment to appreciate over the course of their engagement, which it does according to the findings of paper two and Becht et al. (2010).[67]

The empirical results further suggest less institutional ownership in REITs that are part of an index. Although Cready (1994) suggests that fund managers typically have an incentive to buy into stocks affiliated with an index, institutions do not herd into REITs of the S&P 500. The theory is that institutions invest in index constituents as a form of insurance since institutional portfolio managers are usually evaluated relative to the index and are wary of investing fundamentally differently than their peers (Rajan, 2005), a behavior known as herding. However, institutional investment appears less driven by a REIT's index affiliation. Since herding moves stock prices away from fundamentals (Rajan, 2005), which can contribute to a price bubble, the REIT market benefits from greater prudence of institutional investors in that they invest rather independently from the index. The finding of lower institutional ownership in index-REITs is likely driven by individual investors who favor REITs with greater popularity and analyst coverage. The reasoning is that individuals are typically less sophisticated, trade on "glitter"-stocks and stocks in the news.

[67] The mentioned article finds that abnormal returns of activist funds are more driven by the funds' engagements than by stock picking.

Although the results suggest a preference for underperforming REITs, institutional investors avoid leverage and volatility. Leverage and volatility pose risks that institutions appear unwilling to take. Prior studies do not identify this preference for low leverage and low volatility candidates in the REIT market. In fact, leverage turns out to be the most important determinant of institutional ownership in the firm fixed-effects model. Leverage restrictions of many institutional investors are likely to cause this aversion to high risk.

The higher leverage of REITs compared to industrial firms is in line with the widespread view that real estate should be financed with a high level of debt because it typically generates steady and predictable cash flows. However, altering this view appears reasonable considering that REITs reap fewer benefits from debt than stocks: (a) REITs do not benefit from the tax-shield of debt, because they are tax-exempt and (b) REIT managers and owners have few disagreements regarding the use of free cash flows due to the dividend payout requirement, which makes debt less conducive as a disciplinary device. Both arguments draw the expedience of high leverage in the REIT market into question. Institutional investors may well adjust the leverage of their REIT-portfolio in accordance with personal desires, at least to some extent. Most individual investors should also favor lower leverage in REITs because they are typically less sophisticated and, therefore, may not be able to judge the riskiness of their investments.

Hence, REITs should consider rethinking high-leverage strategies, which impair flexibility to obtain financing during a financial crisis. The associated threats do not become immediately obvious in times of an economic upturn, but may severely impair shareholder wealth in times of distress. The costs associated with rebalancing capital structures through equity offerings, after declining asset prices have driven up leverage, are significant. The extensive re-equitization during the financial crisis reflected unfavorably on the REIT industry. A more conservative capital structure could have limited some of the adverse effects. Therefore, we encourage an intensive debate about and further examination of the capital structure of REITs in the future.

Still, the impact of leverage on return on equity is undisputed and the potential for opportunistic use of leverage is present as discussed in paper one. Institutional investors may play an essential role in determining what leverage strategy to choose. Individual investors are generally smaller and less sophisticated, trading typically less on information and more for speculative reasons (Barber and Odean, 2008; Barber et al., 2009; Chiang et al., 2010). They are unlikely able to critically assess managerial behavior. Institutional investors, however, are more sophisticated, and have access to management and inside information and may, therefore, have the power to discipline management (Becht et al., 2010; Ramalingegowda and Yu, 2011). Institutional investor activism is even more important for REITs than for industrial firms because the market for corporate control of REITs is limited due to ownership restrictions related to the "five or fewer" rule. Institutional investors, therefore, should continue to be a driving force in stabilizing the REIT market, ensuring corporate governance and monitoring managerial actions to promote sustainability and to reestablish trust in the financial sector that has partially forfeited confidence through much publicized opportunistic management and sometimes even fraudulent actions.

We encourage further research on corporate governance in the REIT sector. Building upon our contribution on institutional monitoring as a corporate governance mechanism, research could extend this knowledge by studying the impacts of other factors conducive to corporate governance, such as board structures, compensation schemes, disclosure and reporting requirements as well as regulations and laws. In addition, a careful matching of industrial firms and REITs may provide valuable natural experiments that enable the study of special regulations of the REIT market in isolation. As the effects of the corporate governance mechanisms become more understood, we suggest joint examinations of the mechanisms to identify interactions. Such inferences could contribute to the existing body of the literature by deducing equilibria and effective combinations of compensation, incentivization, control, monitoring, disclosure and regulation to enhance the sustainability of corporate governance structures. The realization of this objective may promote credibility, trust and compliance within capital markets and an increase in efficiency and transparency.

Bibliography

Adams, R. B., Almeida, H. and Ferreira, D. (2005). Powerful CEOs and Their Impact on Corporate Performance. *Review of Financial Studies* **18**(4), 1403-1432.

Adams, R. B. and Ferreira, D. (2007). A Theory of Friendly Boards. *Journal of Finance* **62**(1), 217-250.

Admati, A. R. and Pfleiderer, P. (2009). The "Wall Street Walk" and Shareholder Activism: Exit as a Form of Voice. *Review of Financial Studies* **22**(7), 2645-2685.

Admati, A. R., Pfleiderer, P. and Zechner, J. (1994). Large Shareholder Activism, Risk Sharing, and Financial Market Equilibrium. *Journal of Political Economy* **102**(6), 1097-1130.

Altman, E. I. (1984). A Further Empirical Investigation of the Bankruptcy Cost Question. *Journal of Finance* **39**(4), 1067-1089.

Ambrose, B. W. and Linneman, P. (2001). REIT Organizational Structure and Operating Characteristics. *Journal of Real Estate Research* **21**(3), 141-162.

Ang, J. S., Cole, R. A. and Lin, J. W. (2000). Agency Costs and Ownership Structure. *Journal of Finance* **55**(1), 81-106.

Angrist, J. D. and Pischke, J.-S. (2008). *Mostly Harmless Econometrics: An Empiricist's Companion.* New Jersey, Princeton University Press

Badrinath, S. G., Gay, G. D. and Kale, J. R. (1989). Patterns of Institutional Investment, Prudence, and the Managerial 'Safety-Net' Hypothesis. *Journal of Risk & Insurance* **56**(4), 605-629.

Baker, M. and Wurgler, J. (2002). Market Timing and Capital Structure. *Journal of Finance* **57**(1), 1-32.

Barber, B. M., Lee, Y.-T., Liu, Y.-J. and Odean, T. (2009). Just How Much Do Individual Investors Lose by Trading? *Review of Financial Studies* **22**(2), 609-632.

Barber, B. M. and Odean, T. (2008). All That Glitters: The Effect of Attention and News on the Buying Behavior of Individual and Institutional Investors. *Review of Financial Studies* **21**(2), 785-818.

Barclay, M. J. and Smith, C. W. (2005). The Capital Structure Puzzle: The Evidence Revisited. *Journal of Applied Corporate Finance* **17**(1), 8-17.

Bauer, R., Eichholtz, P. and Kok, N. (2010). Corporate Governance and Performance: The REIT Effect. *Real Estate Economics* **38**(1), 1-29.

Bebchuk, L., Cohen, A. and Ferrell, A. (2009a). What Matters in Corporate Governance? *Review of Financial Studies* **22**(2), 783-827.

Bebchuk, L. A., Cohen, A. and Spamann, H. (2009b). The Wages of Failure: Executive Compensation at Bear Stearns and Lehman 2000-2008. *Yale Journal on Regulation* **27**, 257-282.

Becht, M., Franks, J., Mayer, C. and Rossi, S. (2010). Returns to Shareholder Activism: Evidence from a Clinical Study of the Hermes UK Focus Fund. *Review of Financial Studies* **23**(3), 3093-3129.

Below, S. D., Kiely, J. K. and McIntosh, W. (1995). An Examination of Informed Traders and the Market Microstructure of Real Estate Investment Trusts. *Journal of Real Estate Research* **10**(3), 335-361.

Below, S. D., Kiely, J. K. and McIntosh, W. (1996). REIT Pricing Efficiency; Should Investors Still Be Concerned? *Journal of Real Estate Research* **12**(3), 397-412.

Below, S. D., Stansell, S. R. and Coffin, M. (2000a). The Determinants of REIT Institutional Ownership: Tests of the CAPM. *Journal of Real Estate Finance & Economics* **21**(3), 263-278.

Below, S. D., Stansell, S. R. and Coffin, M. (2000b). Institutional Investment in REIT Common Stocks: An Examination of the Prudent Man Investment. *Journal of Real Estate Portfolio Management* **6**(2), 113-130.

Bennett, J. A., Sias, R. W. and Starks, L. T. (2003). Greener Pastures and the Impact of Dynamic Institutional Preferences. *Review of Financial Studies* **16**(4), 1203-1238.

Bers, M. and Springer, T. M. (1997). Economies-of-Scale for Real Estate Investment Trusts. *Journal of Real Estate Research* **14**(3), 275-291.

Brealey, R. A., Myers, S. C. and Allen, F. (2008). *Principles of Corporate Finance*. New York, McGraw Hill.

Busse, J. A. and Bollen, N. P. B. (2001). On the Timing Ability of Mutual Fund Managers. *Journal of Finance* **56**(3), 1075-1094.

Cameron, A. C. and Trivedi, P. K. (2005). *Microeconometrics: Methods and Applications*. Cambridge, Cambridge University Press.

Cannon, S. E. and Vogt, S. C. (1995). REITs and Their Management: An Analysis of Organizational Structure, Performance and Management Compensation. *Journal of Real Estate Research* **10**(3), 297-317.

Capozza, D. R. and Seguin, P. J. (2000). Debt, Agency, and Management Contracts in REITs: The External Advisor Puzzle. *Journal of Real Estate Finance & Economics* **20**(2), 91-116.

Carhart, M. M. (1997). On Persistence in Mutual Fund Performance. *Journal of Finance* **52**(1), 57-82.

Carleton, W. T., Nelson, J. M. and Weisbach, M. S. (1998). The Influence of Institutions on Corporate Governance through Private Negotiations: Evidence from TIAA-CREF. *Journal of Finance* **53**(4), 1335-1362.

Chan, S. H., Erickson, J. and Wang, K. (2003). *Real Estate Investment Trusts - Structure, Performance and Investment Opportunities*. New York, Oxford University Press.

Chang, X. I. N. and Dasgupta, S. (2009). Target Behavior and Financing: How Conclusive Is the Evidence? *Journal of Finance* **64**(4), 1767-1796.

Chiang, Y.-M., Qian, Y. and Sherman, A. E. (2010). Endogenous Entry and Partial Adjustment in IPO Auctions: Are Institutional Investors Better Informed? *Review of Financial Studies* **23**(3), 1200-1230.

Ciochetti, B. A., Craft, T. M. and Shilling, J. D. (2002). Institutional Investors' Preferences for REIT Stocks. *Real Estate Economics* **30**(4), 567-593.

Cohen, R. B., Gompers, P. A. and Vuolteenaho, T. (2002). Who Underreacts to Cash-Flow News? Evidence from Trading Between Individuals and Institutions. *Journal of Financial Economics* **66**(2-3), 409-462.

Cready, W. M. (1994). Determinants of Relative Investor Demand for Common Stocks. *Journal of Accounting, Auditing & Finance* **9**(3), 487-507.

Damodaran, A., Damodaran, A., Liu, C. H. and Liu, C. H. (1993). Insider Trading as a Signal of Private Information. *Review of Financial Studies* **6**(1), 79-119.

Daniel, K., Grinblatt, M., Titman, S. and Wermers, R. (1997). Measuring Mutual Fund Performance with Characteristic-Based Benchmarks. *Journal of Finance* **52**(3), 1035-1058.

DeAngelo, H. and Masulis, R. W. (1980). Optimal Capital Structure Under Corporate and Personal Taxation. *Journal of Financial Economics* **8**(1), 3-29.

Donaldson, G. (1961). *Corporate Debt Capacity: A Study of Corporate Debt Policy and the Determination of Corporate Debt Capacity.* Boston, Division of Research, Harvard Graduate School of Business Administration.

Eakins, S. G., Stansell, S. R. and Below, S. D. (1996). The Determinants of Institutional Demand for Common Stock: Tests of the CAPM vs. Individual. *International Review of Financial Analysis* **5**(3), 237-257.

Eakins, S. G., Stansell, S. R. and Wertheim, P. E. (1998). Institutional Portfolio Composition: An Examination of the Prudent Investment Hypothesis. *Quarterly Review of Economics & Finance* **38**(1), 93-109.

Edmans, A. and Manso, G. (2011). Governance Through Trading and Intervention: A Theory of Multiple Blockholders. *Review of Financial Studies* **24**(7), 2395-2428.

Eichholtz, P. and Kok, N. (2008). How Does the Market for Corporate Control Function for Property Companies? *Journal of Real Estate Finance & Economics* **36**(2), 141-163.

Fama, E. F. (1980). Agency Problems and the Theory of the Firm. *Journal of Political Economy* **88**(2), 288-307.

Fama, E. F. (1998). Market Efficiency, Long-Term Returns, and Behavioral Finance. *Journal of Financial Economics* **49**(3), 283-306.

Fama, E. F. and French, K. R. (1992). The Cross-Section of Expected Stock Returns. *Journal of Finance* **47**(2), 427-465.

Fama, E. F. and French, K. R. (1993). Common Risk Factors in the Returns on Stocks and Bonds. *Journal of Financial Economics* **33**(1), 3-56.

Fama, E. F. and French, K. R. (2002). Testing Trade-Off and Pecking Order Predictions About Dividends and Debt. *The Review of Financial Studies* **15**(1), 1-33.

Fama, E. F. and French, K. R. (2004). The Capital Asset Pricing Model: Theory and Evidence. *Journal of Economic Perspectives* **18**(3), 25-46.

Fama, E. F. and French, K. R. (2005). Financing decisions: who issues stock? *Journal of Financial Economics* **76**(3), 549-582.

Fama, E. F. and French, K. R. (2010). Luck versus Skill in the Cross Section of Mutual Fund Returns. *Journal of Finance* **65**(5), 1915-1947.

Fama, E. F. and Jensen, M. C. (1983). Separation of Ownership and Control. *Journal of Law and Economics* **26**(June), 301-325.

Fama, E. F. and MacBeth, J. D. (1973). Risk, Return, and Equilibrium: Empirical Tests. *Journal of Political Economy* **81**(3), 607-636.

Feng, Z., Ghosh, C., He, F. and Sirmans, C. (2010). Institutional Monitoring and REIT CEO Compensation. *Journal of Real Estate Finance & Economics* **40**(4), 446-479.

Feng, Z., Price, S. M. and Sirmans, C. F. (2011). An Overview of Equity Real Estate Investment Trusts (REITs): 1993-2009. *Journal of Real Estate Literature* **19**(2), 307-343.

Finnerty, J. E. and Park, H. Y. (1991). Does Managerial Compensation Affect REIT Characteristics? *ORER Letter Series* **1991**, 8-9.

Flannery, M. J. and Rangan, K. P. (2006). Partial adjustment toward target capital structures. *Journal of Financial Economics* **79**(3), 469-506.

Frank, M. Z. and Goyal, V. K. (2009). Capital Structure Decisions: Which Factors Are Reliably Important? *Financial Management* **38**(1), 1-37.

Garrigan, R. T. and Parsons, J. F. C. (1998). *Real Estate Investment Trusts.* New York, McGraw-Hill.

Ghosh, A., Giambona, E., Harding, J. P. and Sirmans, C. F. (2011). How Entrenchment, Incentives and Governance Influence REIT Capital Structure. *Journal of Real Estate Finance & Economics* **43**(1), 39-72.

Ghosh, C. and Sirmans, C. F. (2003). Board Independence, Ownership Structure and Performance: Evidence from Real Estate Investment Trusts. *Journal of Real Estate Finance & Economics* **26**(2/3), 287-318.

Glascock, J. L., Chiuling, L. and So, R. W. (2002). REIT Returns and Inflation: Perverse or Reverse Causality Effects? *Journal of Real Estate Finance & Economics* **24**(3), 301-317.

Glascock, J. L., Hughes Jr, W. T. and Varshney, S. B. (1998). Analysis of REIT IPOs Using a Market Microstructure Approach: Anomalous Behavior or Asset Structure. *Journal of Real Estate Finance & Economics* **16**(3), 243-256.

Gompers, P., Ishii, J. and Metrick, A. (2003). Corporate Governance and Equity Prices. *Quarterly Journal of Economics* **118**(1), 107-155.

Gompers, P. A. and Metrick, A. (2001). Institutional Investors and Equity Prices. *Quarterly Journal of Economics* **116**(1), 229-259.

Grinblatt, M. and Titman, S. (1989). Mutual Fund Performance: An Analysis of Quarterly Portfolio Holdings. *Journal of Business* **62**(3), 393-416.

Grinblatt, M. and Titman, S. (1993). Performance Measurement without Benchmarks: An Examination of Mutual Fund Returns. *Journal of Business* **66**(1), 47-68.

Grinblatt, M., Titman, S. and Wermers, R. (1995). Momentum Investment Strategies, Portfolio Performance, and Herding: A Study of Mutual Fund Behavior. *American Economic Review* **85**(5), 1088-1105.

Harrison, D., Panasian, C. and Seiler, M. J. (2011). Further Evidence on the Capital Structure of REITs. *Real Estate Economics* **39**(1), 133-166.

Howe, J. S. and Shilling, J. D. (1990). REIT Advisor Performance. *Journal of the American Real Estate & Urban Economics Association* **18**(4), 479-500.

Jenkins, J. W. (1980). Incentive Compensation and REIT Financial Leverage and Asset Risk. *Financial Management* **9**(1), 81-87.

Jensen, M. C. (1989). Eclipse of the Public Corporation. *Harvard Business Review* **67**(5), 61-74.

Jensen, M. C. (1993). The Modern Industrial Revolution, Exit, and the Failure of Internal Control Systems. *Journal of Finance* **48**(3), 831-880.

Jensen, M. C. and Meckling, W. H. (1976). Theory of the firm: Managerial behavior, agency costs and ownership structure. *Journal of Financial Economics* **3**(4), 305-360.

John, T. A. and John, K. (1993). Top-Management Compensation and Capital Structure. *Journal of Finance* **48**(3), 949-974.

Kahn, C. and Winton, A. (1998). Ownership Structure, Speculation, and Shareholder Intervention. *Journal of Finance* **53**(1), 99-129.

Leary, M. T. and Roberts, M. R. (2005). Do Firms Rebalance Their Capital Structures? *Journal of Finance* **60**(6), 2575-2619.

Leary, M. T. and Roberts, M. R. (2010). The Pecking Order, Debt Capacity, and Information Asymmetry. *Journal of Financial Economics* **95**(3), 332-355.

Lemmon, M. L., Roberts, M. R. and Zender, J. F. (2008). Back to the Beginning: Persistence and the Cross-Section of Corporate Capital Structure. *Journal of Finance* **63**(4), 1575-1608.

Leuz, C., Lins, K. V. and Warnock, F. E. (2010). Do Foreigners Invest Less in Poorly Governed Firms? *Review of Financial Studies* **23**(3), 3245-3285.

Lewellen, J. (2011). Institutional Investors and the Limits of Arbitrage. *Journal of Financial Economics* **102**(1), 62-80.

Maug, E. (1998). Large Shareholders as Monitors: Is There a Trade-Off between Liquidity and Control? *Journal of Finance* **53**(1), 65-98.

Miller, M. H. (1977). Debt and Taxes. *Journal of Finance* **32**, 261-275.

Modigliani, F. and Miller, M. H. (1958). The Cost of Capital, Corporate Finance and the Theory of Investment. *American Economic Review* **48**(3), 261-297.

Modigliani, F. and Miller, M. H. (1963). Corporate Income Taxes and the Cost of Capital: A Correction. *American Economic Review*, American Economic Association. **53:** 433-443.

Morck, R. and Yeung, B. (2010). Agency Problems and the Fate of Capitalism. *National Bureau of Economic Research Working Paper Series* **No. 16490**.

Morgan, D. P. (2002). Rating Banks: Risk and Uncertainty in an Opaque Industry. *American Economic Review* **92**(4), 874-888.

Myers, S. C. (1984). The Capital Structure Puzzle. *Journal of Finance* **39**(3), 575-592.

Myers, S. C. and Majluf, N. S. (1984). Corporate Financing and Investment Decisions When Firms Have Information That Investors Do Not Have. *Journal of Financial Economics* **13**(2), 187-221.

Nofsinger, J. R. and Sias, R. W. (1999). Herding and Feedback Trading by Institutional and Individual Investors. *Journal of Finance* **54**(6), 2263-2295.

Ooi, J., Seow-Eng, O. and Lin, L. (2010). An Analysis of the Financing Decisions of REITs: The Role of Market Timing and Target Leverage. *Journal of Real Estate Finance & Economics* **40**(2), 130-160.

Ott, S. H., Riddiough, T. J. and Ha-Chin, Y. (2005). Finance, Investment and Investment Performance: Evidence from the REIT Sector. *Real Estate Economics* **33**(1), 203-235.

Petersen, M. A. (2009). Estimating Standard Errors in Finance Panel Data Sets: Comparing Approaches. *Review of Financial Studies* **22**(1), 435-480.

Rajan, R. G. (2005). Has Financial Development Made the World Riskier? *NBER Working Papers* **11728**.

Ramalingegowda, S. and Yu, Y. (2011). Institutional Ownership and Conservatism. *Journal of Accounting & Economics (JAE), Forthcoming.*

Sagalyn, L. B. (1996). Conflicts of Interest in the Structure of REITs. *Real Estate Finance* **13**(2), 34-51.

Shleifer, A. and Vishny, R. W. (1986). Large Shareholders and Corporate Control. *Journal of Political Economy* **94**(3), 461-488.

Shleifer, A. and Vishny, R. W. (1997). A Survey of Corporate Governance. *Journal of Finance* **52**(2), 737-783.

Sias, R. W. (2004). Institutional Herding. *Review of Financial Studies* **17**(1), 165-206.

Sias, R. W., Starks, L. T. and Titman, S. (2006). Changes in Institutional Ownership and Stock Returns: Assessment and Methodology. *Journal of Business* **79**(6), 2869-2910.

Skoulakis, G. (2006). Panel Data Inference in Finance: Least-Squares vs Fama-MacBeth. http://ssrn.com/paper=1108865.

Smith, M. P. (1996). Shareholder Activism by Institutional Investors: Evidence from CalPERS. *Journal of Finance* **51**(1), 227-252.

Su Han, C., Wai Kin, L. and Ko, W. (1998). Institutional Investment in REITs: Evidence and Implications. *Journal of Real Estate Research* **16**(3), 357-374.

Taleb, N. N. (2007). *The Black Swan: The Impact of the Highly Improbable.* New York.

Wang, K., Erickson, J. and Chan, S. H. (1995a). Does the REIT Stock Market Resemble the General Stock Market? *Journal of Real Estate Research* **10**(4), 445-460.

Wang, K., Erickson, J., Gau, G. and Su Han, C. (1995b). Market Microstructure and Real Estate Returns. *Real Estate Economics* **23**(1), 85-100.

Welch, I. (2004). Capital Structure and Stock Returns. *Journal of Political Economy* **112**(1), 106-131.

Welch, I. (2007). Common Flaws in Empirical Capital Structure Research. http://ssrn.com/paper=931675.

Appendix

Appendix 1: Reasons for Institutional Ownership Exceeding 100%

The data on institutional ownership contain the special case of values in excess of 100%. The following explanation names reasons that constitute such rare exceptions. The information is provided by SNL Financial.

Double counting - On the 13-F filing, each institutional holder must report all securities over which they exercise sole or shared investment discretion. In cases where investment discretion is shared by more than one institution double counting may occur. Another cause of double counting is a company name change for the 13F filer where the holdings are accounted for under both filer names.

Short Interest - A large short interest amount affects the institutional ownership amount considerably because all shares that have been sold short appear as holdings in two separate portfolios. One institution has lent its shares to a short seller, while another reporting institution has purchased the same shares. Consequently, the institutional ownership percentage reflected in the 13-F filings is overstated as a percentage of total shares outstanding.

A gap between 'as of' dates - In the case where gaps between the 'as of' dates of the holdings and the shares outstanding arise, the percentage owned could be skewed due to a sharp increase/decrease in shares out.

Other possible reasons:

a) An overlap occurs amongst reporting institutions;

b) The 13F filing includes holdings other than common stock issues;

c) Mutual fund money is co-advised and incorrectly reported by multiple institutions.

Appendix 2: Models With Actual Macroeconomic Data Instead of Expected Data

	Property Type Fixed-Effects	Firm Fixed-Effects
GDP Growth	-2.141***	-0.215
	(0.005)	(0.571)
Interest Rate	1.030	0.300
	(0.158)	(0.494)
Unemployment	-1.224	-0.358
	(0.109)	(0.303)
Inflation	0.002*	-0.000
	(0.100)	(0.897)
Excess Market Return	-0.055**	-0.017
	(0.012)	(0.204)
Trend	0.016***	0.008***
	(0.000)	(0.000)
Leverage	-0.123	-0.233***
	(0.106)	(0.000)
Market-to-Book	-0.000	-0.005
	(0.982)	(0.247)
Size	0.151***	-0.020
	(0.000)	(0.688)
Asset Tangibility	-0.101	-0.122
	(0.512)	(0.172)
Profitability	-1.916**	-0.572**
	(0.027)	(0.030)
Earnings Volatility	0.009**	0.004*
	(0.033)	(0.074)
Stock Volatility	-0.069	-0.180*
	(0.816)	(0.067)
Beta	0.022	-0.006
	(0.343)	(0.434)
Dividend Payout	-0.112***	-0.011
	(0.004)	(0.410)
Δ Stock Price	-0.001	-0.028**
	(0.971)	(0.012)
Rating	0.059	-0.018
	(0.144)	(0.441)
S&P 500 Constituency	-0.088**	-0.040*
	(0.038)	(0.065)
Constant	-1.297***	0.395
	(0.001)	(0.399)
Adjusted R^2	0.441	0.910

Notes: The table presents coefficients and p-values in parentheses of fixed-effects regressions including 3885 observations with *institutional ownership* as the dependent variable. Different to our base models in Table 17 we use actual macroeconomic data instead of expected data. *GDP Growth* is the change in US gross domestic product, *interest rate* is the 10-Year Treasury Note rate and *Inflation* is the change in the CPI. Standard errors are robust to heteroscedasticity and autocorrelation. * indicates significance at the 10% level, ** indicates significance at the 5% level, *** indicates significance at the 1% level.

Appendix 3: Illustration of Variance Contributions - Macroeconomic Factors

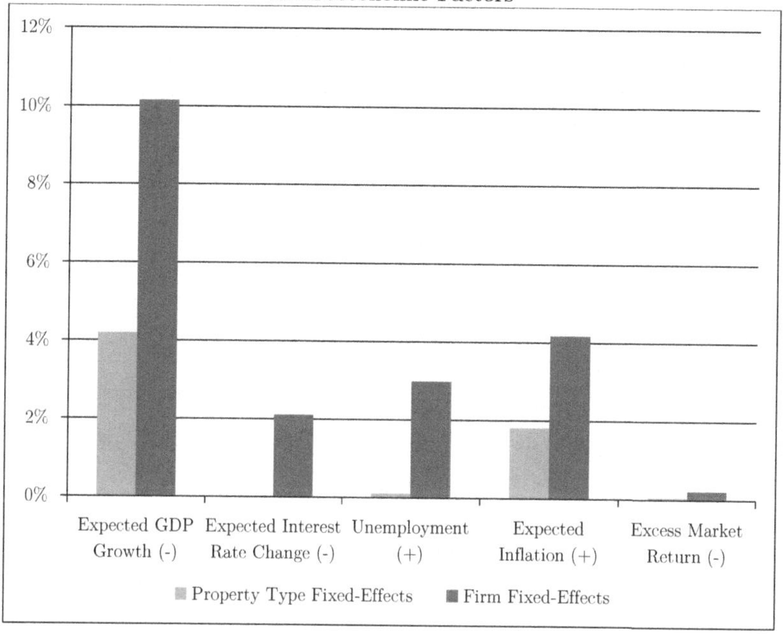

Notes: The chart presents the quotient of each effect's partial sum of squares divided by the total sum of squares of all factors in percent. The partial sum of squares of each effect is divided by the total sum of squares of all factors (except the fixed-effects and the *trend* variable) to force the columns to sum to one. This identifies the fraction of sum of squares that are attributable to one particular effect. The sign in parentheses following the variable name describes whether the impact on institutional ownership is positive (+) or negative (-).

Appendix 4: Illustration of Variance Contributions - REIT Characteristics

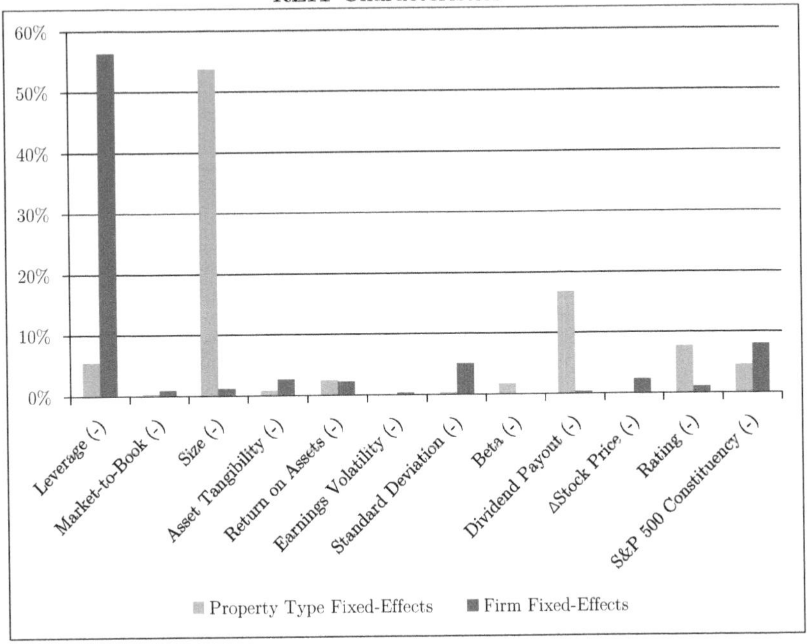

Notes: The chart presents the quotient of each effect's partial sum of squares divided by the total sum of squares of all factors in percent. The partial sum of squares of each effect is divided by the total sum of squares of all factors (except the fixed-effects and the *trend* variable) to force the columns to sum to one. This identifies the fraction of sum of squares that are attributable to one particular effect. The sign in parentheses following the variable name describes whether the impact on institutional ownership is positive (+) or negative (-).

Appendix 5: Elasticities of Covariates - Macroeconomic Factors

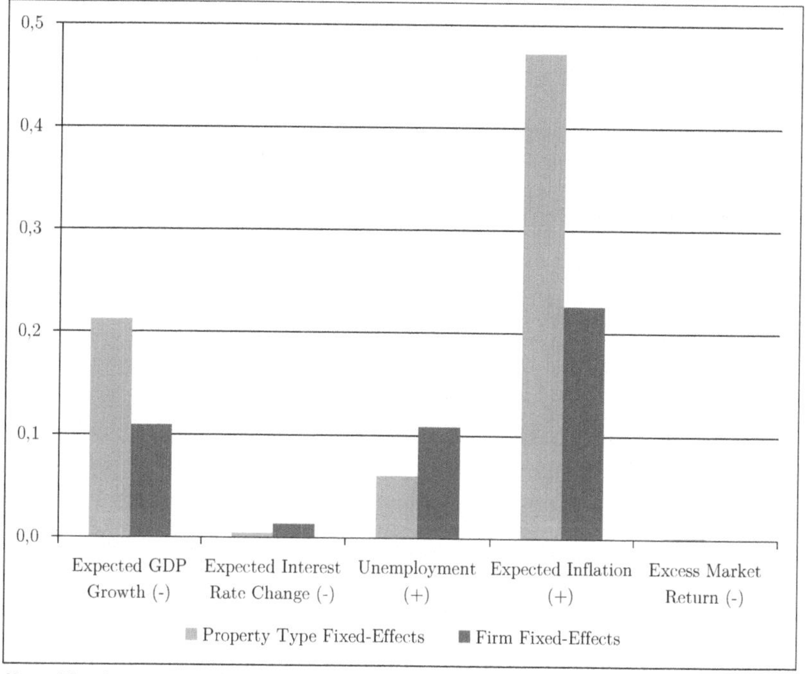

Notes: The chart presents absolute values of the elasticities of the covariates at their means. The sign in parentheses following the variable name describes whether the impact on institutional ownership is positive (+) or negative (-).

Appendix 6: Elasticities of Covariates - REIT Characteristics

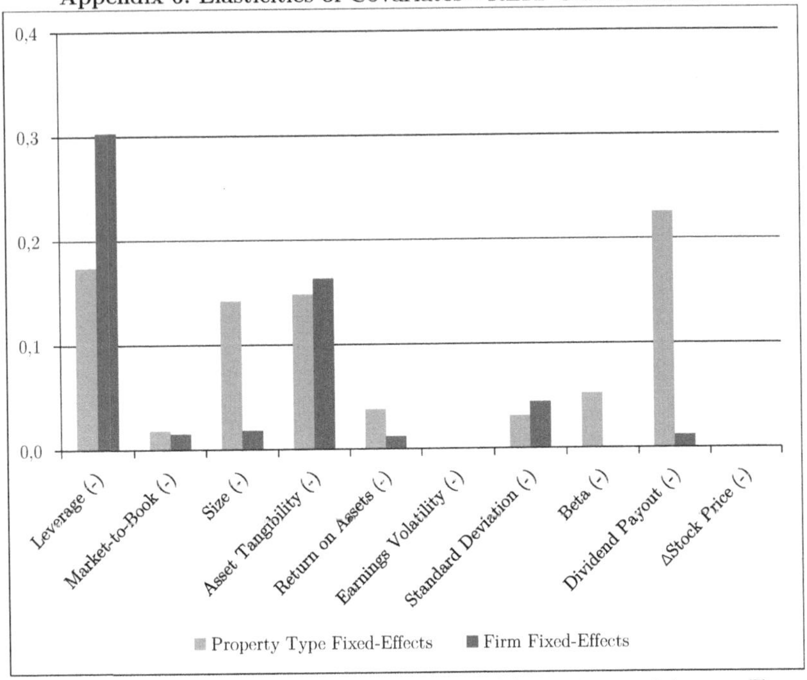

Notes: The chart presents absolute values of the elasticities of the covariates at their means. The sign in parentheses following the variable name describes whether the impact on institutional ownership is positive (+) or negative (-).

The manufacturer's authorised representative in the EU is Springer Nature Customer Service Centre GmbH, Europaplatz 3, 69115 Heidelberg, Germany. If you have any concerns regarding our products, please contact ProductSafety@springernature.com

Printed and bound by CPI Group (UK) Ltd, Croydon, CR0 4YY
22/09/2026
02221067-0017